Magic Mantras to a Pain-Free Back

Dr Yatish Agarwal (MBBS, MD, DSc) is a renowned physician, writer and columnist. His popular books, articles, columns, and radio and TV programmes have spread the message of good health and sensible living to millions of people. Many of his works are available in a number of languages. Bestowed with several national awards, Dr Agarwal works and teaches at New Delhi's Safdarjung Hospital and V.M. Medical College. He has also been a National Consultant to the WHO, and a Fellow at the National Cancer Center Hospital, Tokyo; and Institute of Population and Research, Mahidol University, Thailand. He can be contacted at: dryatish@yahoo.com.

Dr A P Singh [MBBS, D Orth, DNB Orth, Diplome d'Assistant Etranger (France)] is an eminent Orthopaedic and Arthroscopic Surgeon, and a leading expert on spinal disorders. An academician at heart, he has been the President, Gurgaon Orthopaedic Society (2005-10). This work is born out of his three-decade-long experience and expertise as a doctor treating patients with backache. Dr Singh is currently the Medical Director, Uma Sanjeevani Hospitals, DLF City-2 and Sector 55, Gurgaon. In the past, he has worked at the Safdarjung Hospital, New Delhi; St. Louis Hospital, Paris; Massachusetts General Hospital, Boston; and SUNY Medical Centre, Syracuse, New York.

Some other titles by Dr Yatish Agarwal

- All About Having A Baby
- Heartcare
- Bodytalk
- The World Within
- Managing Diabetes: How Much Sugar is Too Much!
- HeartTalk: Your Roadmap to a Healthy Heart
- High Blood Pressure: Tame the Stealth Killer
- The Daily Bread
- The Medicine Chest
- The Story of Blood

Magic Mantras to a Pain-Free Back

Dr Yatish Agarwal
Dr A P Singh

BLUEJAY

Bluejay Books Pvt. Ltd.
A-8/76, Ist Floor, Sector 16
Rohini, Delhi 110 085
info@bluejaybooksindia.com

This edition published by
Bluejay Books Pvt. Ltd 2013

Text set in
Garamond, Swis721, Swiss911,
ChaseCallasSH, and Book Antique.

Printed and bound in India

MAGIC MANTRAS to a Pain-Free Back provides reliable, practical, easy-to-understand information on common back problems, with a focus on self-help. The information and recommendations given in this book are in no way intended to be a substitute for your doctor's advice.

To my son Apoorv,
who sailed through this voyage with me.
His enthusiasm and boundless love
kept me on course.

Yatish Agarwal

To my parents–
Prof. M P Singh & Uma Singh,
who gave me a joyful childhood
and taught me the values of life.

AP Singh

Foreword

Mother Nature's gift of the two-legged erect stance, while putting *Homo sapiens* at an advantage over the rest of the animal kingdom, has also given them a back that is vulnerable to considerable stresses and strains and, consequently, back pain.

The modern push-button age has further conspired with the elements of Nature. If man's intellect and ingenuity have allowed him to produce gadgets to make life easier for him, it has also robbed him of the many joys of life. The modern-day man is besotted with a lifestyle that gives him little opportunity to service the muscles, ligaments, joints and bones of his back. Deprived of natural exercise, put through constant rushes of adrenaline-sparked stress, burdened by protruding belly and having a longer life span, more and more people have begun to complain of bad backs.

People with back problems add up to the largest single group of patients visiting any orthopaedic clinic. Yet, the art and science of treating the back requires a conscientious doctor, who is a good listener, and has the patience to dig into the etiological factors in each patient, and come up with a plan that allows his patients to triumph over their back problems.

Within the pages of this book, you'll find practical advice on how to identify and treat your back problems before they become difficult to manage or hinder the quality of your life. You'll also learn about lifestyle changes that may reduce your risk of developing constant aches and pains in the back.

The book contains a complete section on healing prescriptions. Taking a holistic approach, it educates about good posture, instructs in exercises and yogic postures to strengthen the back, offers homecare remedies in the case of acute back pain, and discusses a wide range of treatment options: medications, surgical treatments and alternative therapies.

The book should prove to be a boon for the common reader. At the same time, it should also interest physicians, who will benefit by acquiring the idiom to communicate more effectively with the patients and their families and also by refreshing their practical knowledge base.

Dr R K Srivastava
MS (Orthopaedics), DNB (Rehabilitation)
Former Director General of Health Services
Government of India

Preface

Back pain is one of the most common health problems in the world. The numbers might vary among different studies, yet 70-90 per cent of people endure back pain at some period of their lives. Thus, if you have back pain, you're not alone. It is the prime cause of disability, and may strike just at the time you are about to peak in life or reap its rewards.

The biggest culprit in the bad back epidemic is modern-day living. From being a creator of machines, man has increasingly become a prey to mechanization. Diminishing opportunities for physical activity and stressful deadlines lead to a backbreaking lifestyle, literally. Robbed of exercise, the spinal muscles go weak; the ligaments that hold the bones and joints in symphony waste away; the joints lose their flexibility; and the vertebral bones suffer wear and tear. So if you tip the scales on the wrong side by playing against the biomechanics of your back and not following the basic rules of back care, you have only yourself to blame. For once the changes become permanent, a bad back can shatter your life's dream.

If you have already started on the road to a bad back, though the clock cannot be turned back, damage control can and should be done.This easy-to-understand book provides reliable information for developing a sturdier back. Within these pages you'll find the 'ounce of prevention that is worth more than a pound of cure'and yes, also the strategies for effecting a cure.

The book gives you a detailed roadmap of back pain management signposted with the fundamentals: back protection, exercise, yogic postures (*asana*), pain control, diet and, perhaps most importantly, how best to maintain a healthier lifestyle.

The section on treatment options discusses a wide range of medications, the latest surgical treatments and also alternative therapies.

A thorough understanding of your problem and the treatment options and, more importantly, the will to put this knowledge to use in daily living will empower you to address and overcome back pain. It would also make for effective communication with your doctor.

Look for a doctor who has the time and empathy to understand your problem, so that he or she can offer lasting relief. The doctor should be capable and diligent in providing a comprehensive diagnosis, accurate answers and effective treatment.

We hope this book will be able to answer the very many, varied and individualistic queries of the sufferers of back problems. However, if there is something more you would like to know, write to us. We would be happy to write back to you. In any case, look up the next edition of the book for further additions.

We wish you the very best for a robust back and a healthier life.

Dr Yatish Agarwal
Dr A P Singh

Measure your health by your sympathy with morning and spring. If there is no response in you to the awakening of Nature – if the prospect of an early morning walk does not banish sleep, if the warble of the first bluebird does not thrill you – know that the morning and spring of your life are past. Thus may you feel your pulse.

–Henry David Thoreau

Contents

Part 3 Fitness Mantras

Part 4 Remedies & Cure

PART ONE

The Wonderful Human Back

The human back is an incredible machine with an amazing design. It is carved out of several small bones called vertebrae, which sit on top of each other in a vertical stack. These bones are held in place by a large number of tough bands called ligaments, several layers of muscles and well-built joints. They provide equilibrium and facilitate a variety of spinal movements.

Sandwiched between each pair of vertebral bones lies a cushion-like disc. It protects the bones from damage, but if pushed out of place, it can put you to serious trouble.

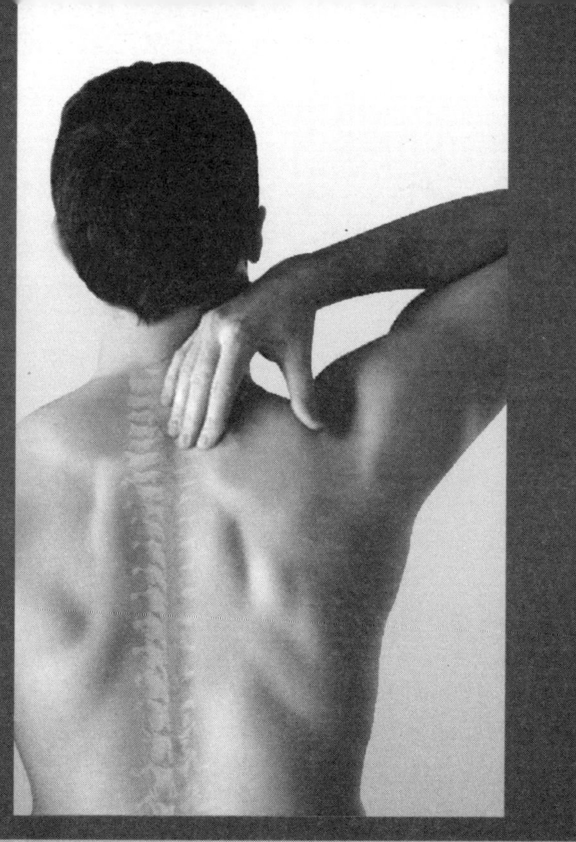

This basic design is enhanced by three eye-catching curves: a graceful forward curve in the neck, a backward directed one in the mid back and a forward curve in the lower back. They provide stability to the vertical pillar of the back.

Within the rock-steady tunnel crafted out of the vertebral bones, runs a neural superhighway called the spinal cord. Crucial to the vital functions of the human body, it picks and carries signals from different organs of the body and delivers the requisite commands to them.

1
The Amazing Back Machine

The tower-like upright human back is a creation of a most amazing kind. Sculpted out of a chain of small bones called vertebrae, it is like a chassis, which holds and fits the different pieces of human body as one.

Think of the body without the spine, and you will find it impossible to piece the human body together. At its top, it holds the skull, which encases your brain. In the neck, it provides the bony frame to several key structures, including the windpipe, the big arteries to the brain, the veins that lug the blood from the head to the heart, the spinal cord, and the thyroid and parathyroid glands. In the chest, it anchors the ribs and offers housing to the heart, lungs and the big vessels. Lower, between the lowest ribs and the pelvis, it provides the case for human body's proverbial Pandora's box, the abdomen.

A bit lower, it articulates with the pelvic bone to form a basin-shaped cavity, the pelvis, which holds the reproductive organs, the urinary bladder, and the terminal portion of the large bowel.

Intimate secrets

Look a little more closely, and you will find that the human backbone consists of 33 pieces of vertebrae, which sit on top of each other in a vertical stack. There are seven in the neck (cervical), 12 in the chest (thoracic) and five in the lower back (lumbar). The base of the spine sits on the sacrum – a triangular block of bone behind the pelvis built by five vertebral pieces glued together.

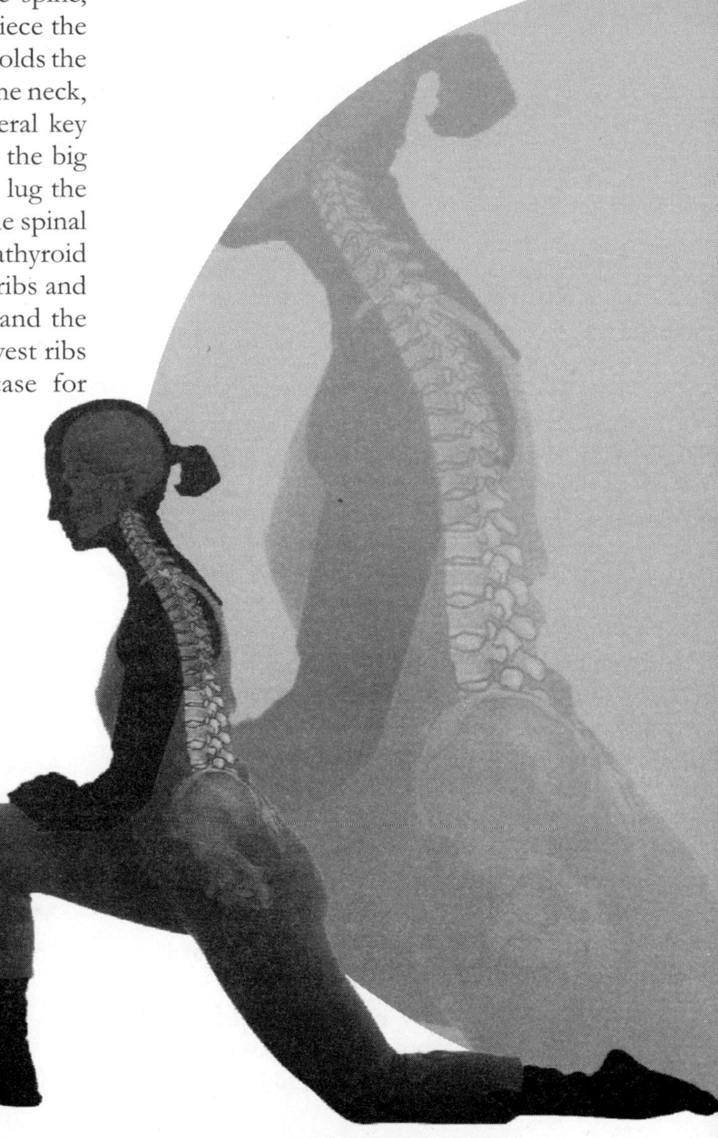

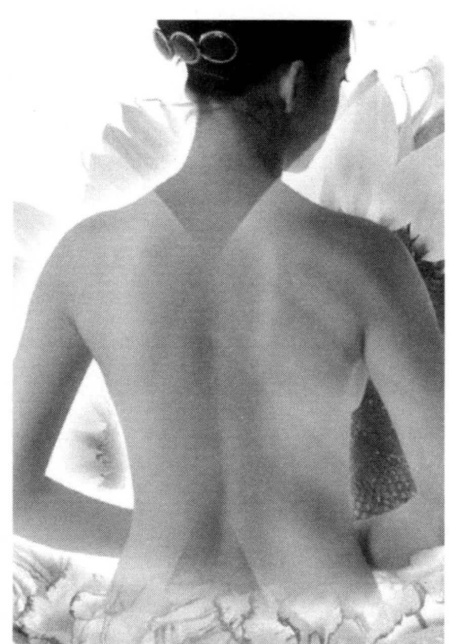

Just below the sacrum, hangs the tailbone coccyx, consisting of four fused rudimentary vertebrae.

Running between the head and the buttocks, the spine rises out of the pelvis in three gentle curves. A hollow in the lower back, a gentle hump in the chest region and a graceful forward arch in the neck. These curvatures provide a degree of resilience to the spinal column that would not be possible in a series of rigid, straightly stacked bones.

A perfectly aligned spinal column achieves two ends: it ensures the proper distribution of body weight through the front and back compartments of the spine and allows the lower back to bend forward slightly to absorb impact while walking.

You may ask why is the backbone called so? The answer is surprisingly simple: just because it runs on the rear side of the human frame. Before we go any further, let's take a closer look at the basic design of the vertebral bones.

A masterly design

While vertebrae in each region have their peculiarities, they have a common basic design. They are shaped somewhat like a ring. They have a body or a large mass of solid bone in front set like a diamond on a ring; and twin arches which curve backwards on each side of the body to form a circular opening behind.

This simple design works wonderfully well for the spinal column. While the stout bodies of the vertebrae carry body's weight, a perfect tunnel is formed behind where the circular openings in the vertebral bodies line with each other. This tunnel is called the neural canal, and it serves as a housing for the spinal cord.

Parts of a typical vertebra

Each vertebra has a solid, weight-bearing section and a hole formed by the vertebral arch, which protects the spinal cord. Projecting bony or transverse processes make contact with those of the vertebrae above and below, and provide anchoring points for the various muscles and ligaments in the back.

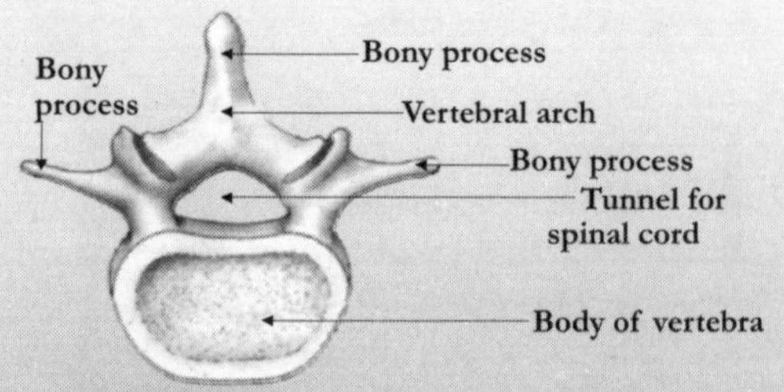

Even though this may seem a bit dull, let's take a closer look at the other bits and pieces of the vertebra. On each side, just where the bony arch begins to curve backward, a horizontal projection crops up. It is called the transverse process.

On the outer side of each vertebral arch, both on its top surface and the bottom surface, a set of bony projections called articular processes arise. They meet with the articular processes of the adjoining vertebrae. These joints help maintain some degree of movement between the vertebrae.

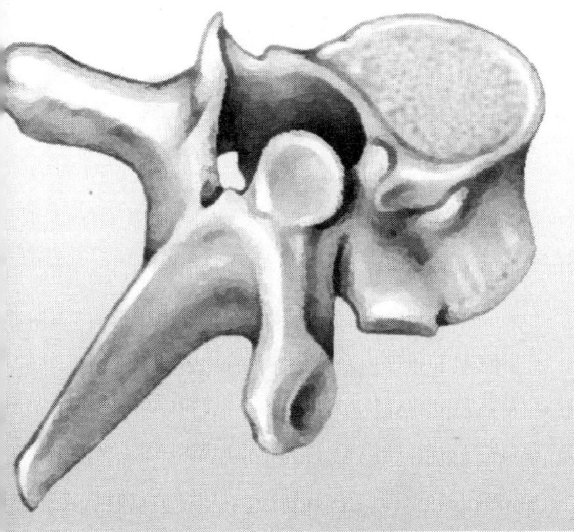

As the vertebral arches curve further backwards, the two arches meet in the midline. Here, another bony projection arises to project back. It is called the spine. Spines act as levers for muscles which extend the vertebral column or, to a lesser extent, rotate it. These vertebral appendages help link and couple the vertebrae into a strong, stable and efficient column.

A test of mobility

Now, let us try and discover the mobility quotient of different portions of the spinal column. The neck, which consists of seven vertebrae, is capable of a most extraordinary range of movements. Not only does it support the all-important head, the shape of the neck bones and their articulations are such as to help look down at the ground or up at the stars in an instant. Also, the head can be turned 180 degrees from side to side to glance over either shoulder – a movement required to look suddenly behind while reversing the car, or before crossing a busy street.

The 12 thoracic or chest vertebrae that follow, are not quite capable of as wide a range of movement as the neck is. Only slight twisting and backward tilting are possible in this part. This limitation is imparted by the 12 pairs of ribs hooked on each of the 12 vertebrae.

At the lower end are five heavy lumbar vertebrae, which carry most of the body's weight. They permit a wide range of movements. If you wish to check, carry out a few exercises. First, sit on a stool and place both hands on the back of your head. Now, twist yourself at the waist, first one way and then the other, taking care that the hips do not move. Next stand straight with the feet slightly apart. Remember the good old school days? Now bend sideways and try to reach down, sliding one hand down the thigh and knee as far down as the leg and ankle. Finally, test your forward bending range by trying to touch the feet without bending the knees. Similarly, test the backward arch by extending the arms up and carrying them back while tilting back at the waist. You would agree the lumbar spine allows a reasonable extent of movements.

This little tour down the spinal column is about to end, and simply because of biological evolution, with a whimper. Since the lowermost bones, the sacrum and the coccyx, are fused, this is the least mobile area of the spine as practically no movement is possible in this segment. Step down the evolution ladder, and you would find that our nearest cousins, the apes, use the tail as an additional piece of their locomotion apparatus.

The purposeful curves

When we are born, the spine has just one long single forward-facing curve and is shaped like a comma from the head to the tail.

On becoming a toddler, we acquire a second backward-facing curve at the waist. As a result, the spinal column takes a gentle S-shape.

While these curves make the human figure more attractive, they are not without purpose. The S-shape arch that they form acts as a vital shock absorber. It cushions the impact of millions of jolts that the spine receives while doing its normal daily chores like turning, sitting, rising, standing, walking, jumping, and running.

Cushions for the back

Sandwiched between each pair of successive vertebral bones, the spine is endowed with special cushions called intervertebral discs. They insulate the vertebral bones from wear and tear.

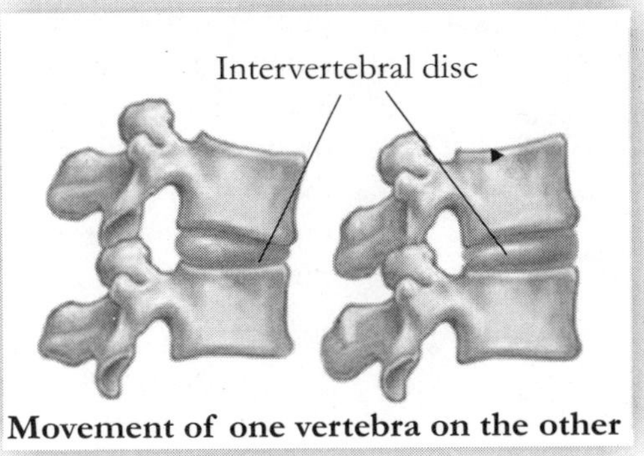

Movement of one vertebra on the other

Without them, each vertebra may ground the other, and the vertebral column may suffer quick damage.

The spinal column is gifted with 23 intervertebral discs. Since the top two vertebrae – the first and second neck vertebrae – in the spinal column are specialized to allow the head a greater range of movement than would be possible with the normal vertebrae, they have been provided with a stable ball-and-socket joint which accommodates both side-to-side and up-and-down motion. This negates the need for an intervertebral disc between them. Likewise, for an altogether different reason, the five fused pieces of sacrum and the four of the tailbone are also not provided with the intervertebral discs. That's because they lack movement.

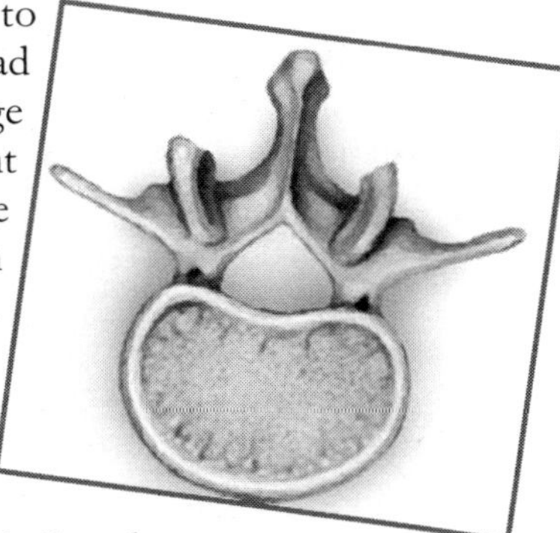

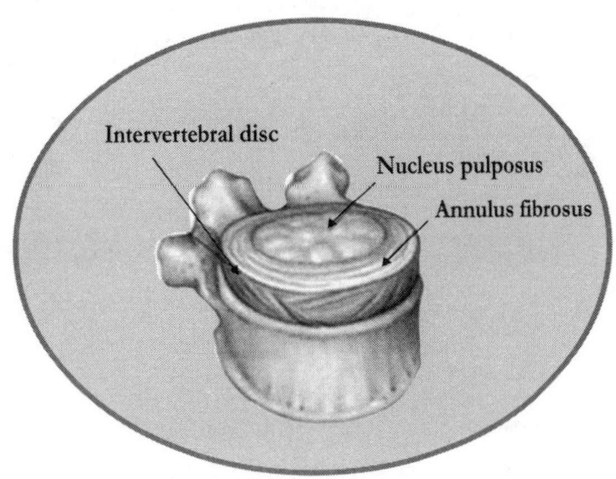

The structure of the intervertebral discs is also well designed. Each intervertebral disc consists of a hard outer shell called the *annulus fibrosus*, and has a jelly-like filling in the middle, the *nucleus pulposus*. The disc can swell and shrink, and can change its consistency. It does so by imbibing or squeezing out fluid through tiny holes in the tough plates of the tissue placed above and below the disc.

The annulus fibrosus or the tough outer capsule of the disc consists of obliquely arranged fibres. They help maintain the strength and integrity of the disc when the spine is put to twisting stress and strain. Yet, this tough shell of the disc has a chink in its armour – its rear portion has a weak spot.

Standing up to the stresses and strains of daily life, by the age of 20, intervertebral discs begin to lose their elasticity. The wear and tear process in the discs sets in quite early. With no nerve supply and a poor blood supply, this degenerative process is absolutely pain-free. The disc slowly swells up following an injury, yet it shows no inflammatory reaction and makes no attempt to heal. In fact, small pieces of the disc may even break off without giving any pain. Since the rear side of the outer capsule is weak, it is quickest to succumb. Once that happens, the jelly-like nucleus begins to bulge or protrude out, causing pressure on the adjacent spinal structures and the nerve roots. The infamy of the disc relates to this. A slipped or prolapsed disc is one of the commonest problems of the back. The severity of symptoms depends upon the degree of protrusion. If a prolapsed disc impinges the posterior longitudinal ligament, it causes some pain. If the protrusion is large, the disc also presses on the nerves in the spinal canal.

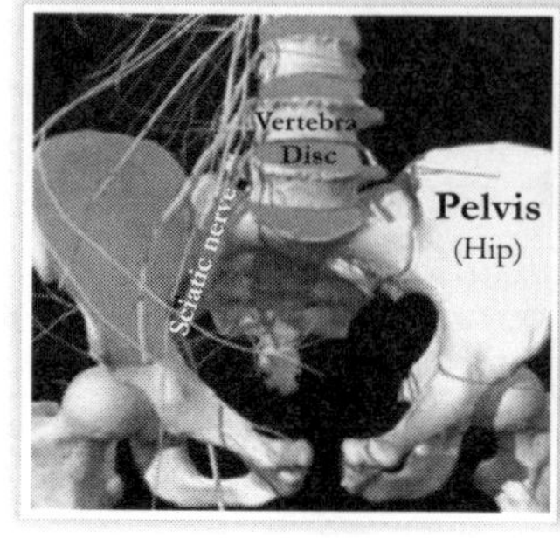

The elastic disc

The compressible nature of your intervertebral discs allows them to deform as you carry a load and then spring back into shape.

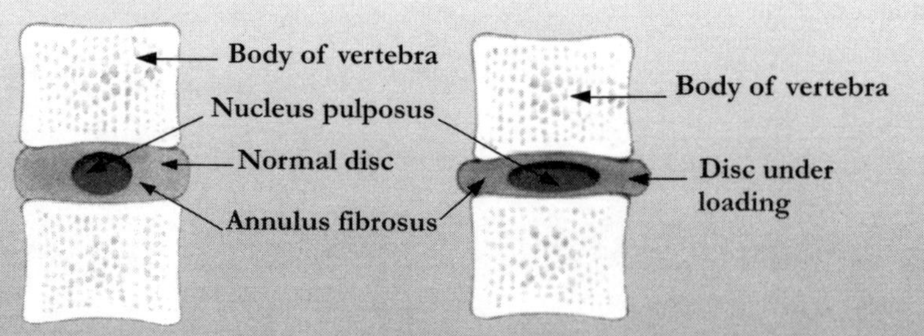

Sometimes, a portion of the disc may prolapse or herniate into the spinal canal, and pinch the nerve roots that pass out of the spinal canal through small openings, called the vertebral foramina, situated one on each side between the two vertebrae. If that happens, the sufferer may feel severe pain along the course of the nerve root, and/or numbness and weakness in the region. When such a situation causes a shooting pain down the back of the thigh, it is called *sciatica*, while a similar pain along the arm is called *brachialgia*.

Binders and movers

An elaborate system of tough bands called ligaments and a number of back and abdominal muscles run up and down the spinal column. They work day in and day out, imparting the backbone strength, stability and mobility.

The ligaments run all along the length of the spine. While the one called the posterior longitudinal ligament runs just behind the back surface of the vertebral bodies and the intervertebral discs, the anterior longitudinal ligament lines the front of the spinal column. These two ligaments bind the vertebral bodies and the intervertebral discs into a strong column.

Short bands called the interspinous ligaments run obliquely between one vertebral spine and the next. Likewise, the intertransverse ligaments extend between the transverse processes of adjoining vertebrae, and the ligamentum flava (*singular*: ligament flavum) help bind the ring-shaped arches of successive vertebral bodies. These ligaments help preserve the fine alignment of the spinal column.

A large number of strong muscles in the back and abdomen work in tandem to stabilise the back and facilitate its movements. These muscles run in layers. The short intervertebral muscles, medium-sized intersegmental muscles, and large paraspinal and abdominal muscles wrap around the spinal column and play a major role in keeping it straight, in moving the vertebrae and maintaining the poise and balance of the body in different postures.

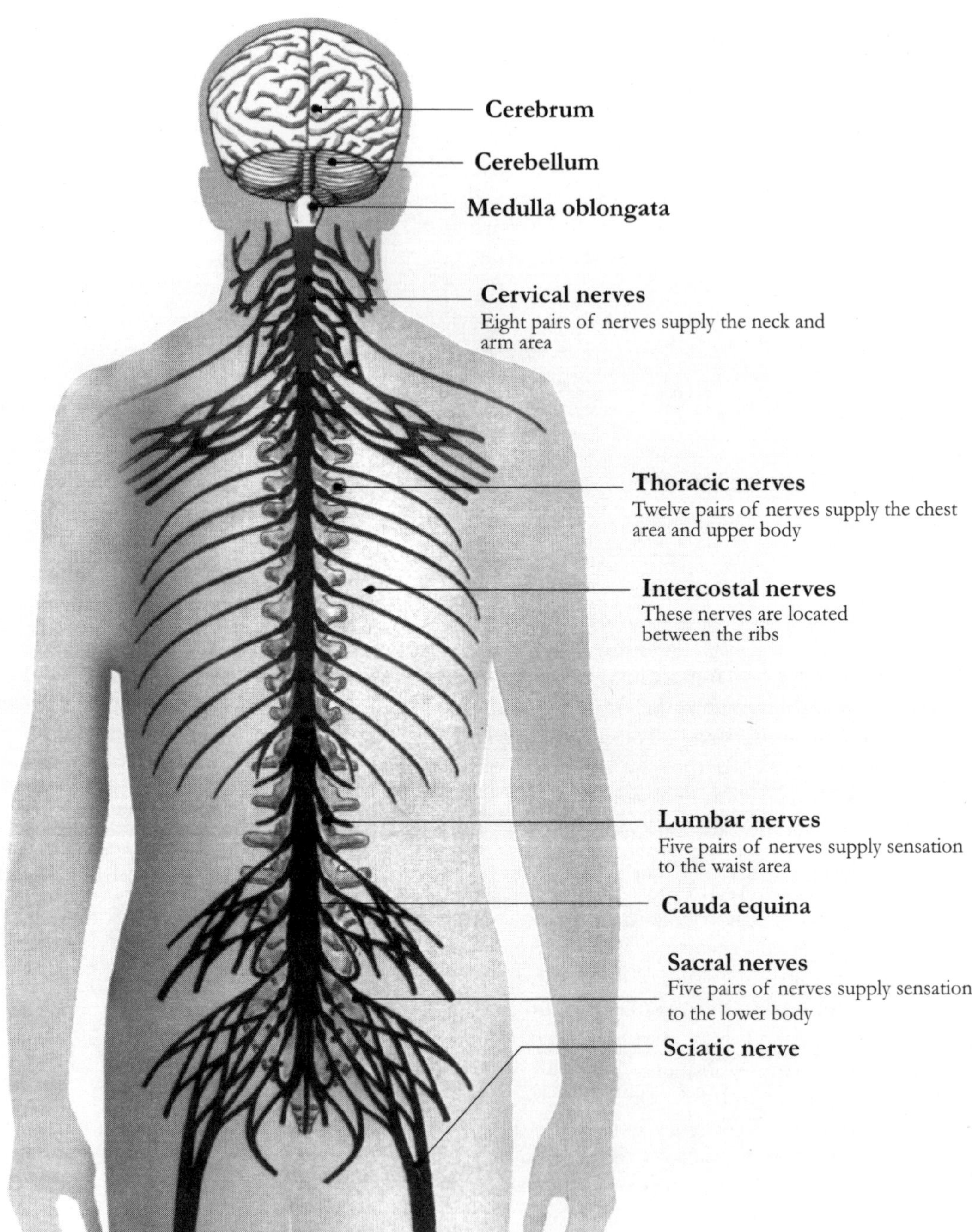

The human body's neural superhighway

The neural superhighway

Within the hollowness of the spinal column formed by consecutive circular openings in the vertebrae runs a secure tunnel, which is a well ensconced home for the spinal cord. This neural superhighway transmits millions of messages between the brain and different parts of the body. The spinal cord distributes 31 pairs of spinal nerves.

While some serve the sensory function and convey information to the brain, the others carry out motor jobs and transmit orders from the brain to the muscles. The spinal nerve roots exit from the spinal canal through narrow openings called *neural foramina*, which are sited between adjoining vertebrae.

Though the motherboard of the human body is located in the brain, the spinal cord is quite capable of quick thinking and taking decisions in extraordinary circumstances. For instance, when your finger touches a hot object, the spinal cord does not even take a second to dictate that the finger be immediately removed.

Within the tunnel, the spinal cord has added protection. It is encased by three layers of tough membranes called meninges and a flowing cerebrospinal fluid. Still, the spinal cord can sometimes suffer damage in injuries of the vertebral column. Road traffic accidents and falls from height are the commonest causes of such injuries. Depending on the degree and level of damage, this may leave the victim paralysed in one, both or all four limbs. However, timely surgery can help many such people.

2
The Incredibly Simple Dynamics

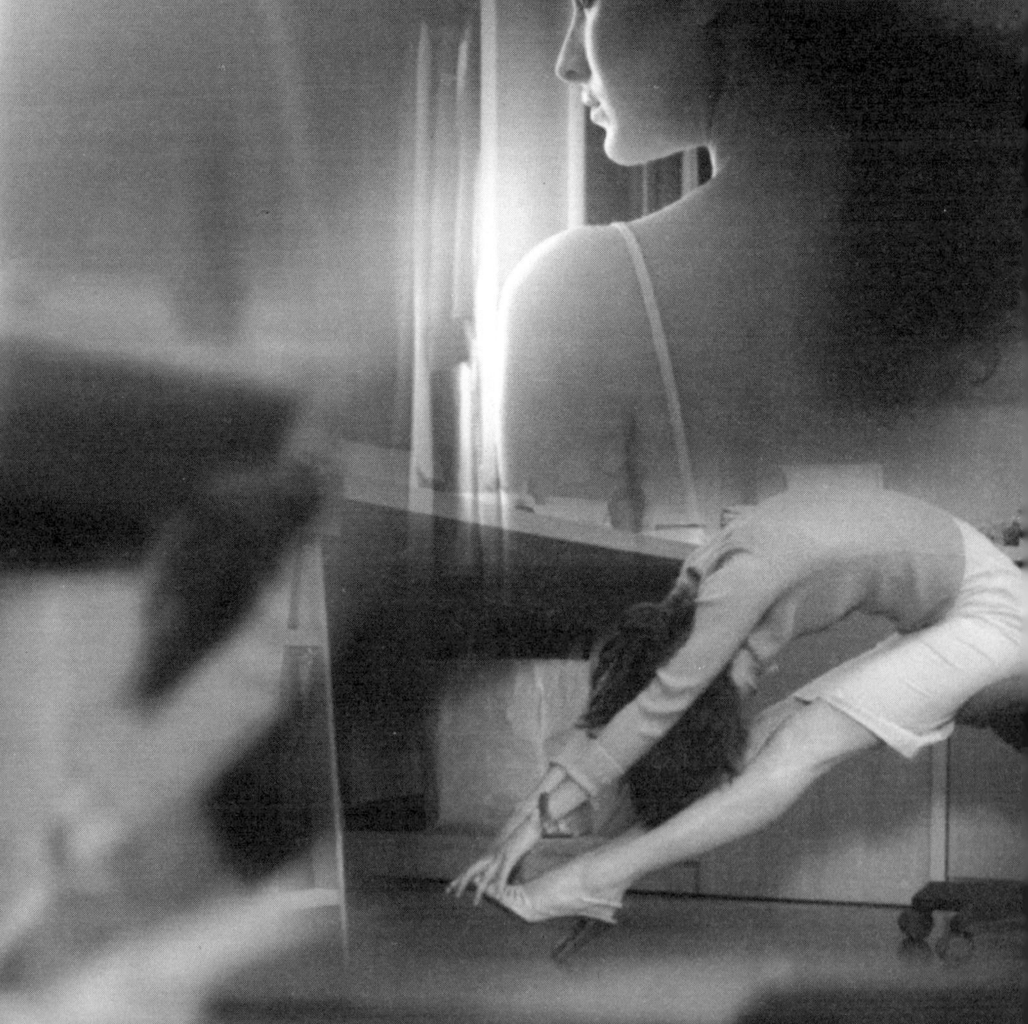

As the fable relates, seven blind men were once asked to describe an elephant. Since they were wise, they decided to feel a pachyderm to form a visual picture in their mind. Yet, since they could not see, each felt a different piece of the elephant's anatomy. Thus, each came up with a different answer. While one compared the elephant to a rope, the second said it was like a tree trunk, the third stated it was akin to a wall, while the fourth equated it with a tent, the fifth to a leaf, the sixth to a horn and the seventh and wisest of them all said it resembled a snake. In fact so sure were they of themselves that they began to quarrel with each other. Rather than being myopic, the need was to reconcile the facts that they had so wisely garnered.

Solving the problems of the back requires a similar sage approach. Over the next few pages, we look into the simple biomechanics of the back, so crucial in tackling the curse of backache.

Preserving the gift

The first humans evolved from our ape ancestors some five million years ago. A major characteristic distinguished them from the apes: the new species was bipedal – that is, it had the ability to walk on two legs. Until then, man's predecessors were all four-legged beings. They had a bridge like design for their back with two pairs of limbs to joist them up. This module worked perfectly well for them as they could fulfil their basic needs for survival and procreation in this flat posture. In any case, their brain was not so developed as to think that a raised head would offer them advantage.

Biologists believe that the first humans walked in a far less an upright manner than us. They perhaps alternated between upright and flat posture, and this probably related to their brain size and intellectual ability. As millennia whizzed by, the human race evolved further. This story of man's evolution is best portrayed in naturalist Charles Darwin's work. As man's cranium became bigger in size and his intelligence grew, his body evolved to maintain an erect posture and two-legged gait.

New biomechanics came into force. Tough bands known as ligaments, which tied the vertebral joints in one unit and kept them in place, also helped in keeping up the spine upright. Not to be left behind, the muscles also powered their way to prop up the body, keep it stable and prevent it from slipping into a flat position. Several back muscles worked in tandem all the time to fulfil this mission.

The modern man, *Homo sapiens* still relies upon these basic biomechanisms to preserve his stance. What was Mother Nature's gift to man, must now be sustained by man himself. If you want to enjoy the gift of being a biped or two-footed being, keep your ligaments and back muscles in shape. Strengthen them so you may be a master of a robust back.

Virtues of staying trim and fit

The abdominal muscles must stay in shape for the spine to be healthy. Weak abdominal muscles burden the lumbar spine with greater stress. To cope with weak muscles, the spine then must arch far too back to maintain its balance. Thus, if you wish to keep your back out of trouble, it's time you began servicing

your tummy muscles. Devote 15 minutes daily to exercises that strengthen your abdominal and back muscles.

You must also watch your weight. If you develop a paunch, your abdominal muscles turn weak. You also tend to burden your backbone, especially the lower back. The muscles that work the back of the spine tend to become far too taut and the back begins to arch more severely. This continuous strain takes a toll. The lower back muscles develop painful knots or lumps. Now and again, put to extra severe strain, they give way. This micro tearing of muscles causes a swelling in the surrounding tissues and worsens the spasm. Over time, this disturbance in biomechanics sparks off greater wear and tear, causing degenerative arthritis or spondylosis in the lumbar spine.

Strong abdominal muscles are your best guarantee against this change. Even if they are put under extra strain, rather than getting torn, they just gently stretch.

Know the trouble spots

A newborn baby has no spinal curves. Until an infant grows and becomes more active, his back is shaped like a comma in one continuous curve. Just like if it was curled up while he nestled in his mother's womb. This primary curve undergoes changes as the infant grows and lifts up his head, tries to sit, crawl, stand and walk. At around three months of age, when the infant tries to lift his head and look around, he begins to develop a forward arch in the neck. By nine months when the child is able to sit, this curve becomes more definite.

Soon the infant celebrates his first birthday. Before long he begins to walk. It is around this time that he develops a hollow in his lower back.

While these curves help support the vertical pillar of the back, they also imperil those vertebral joints where the spinal curvature is most acute. Thus, while in the neck the fifth and sixth cervical vertebrae are the most vulnerable trouble spots, in the lower back the fourth and fifth lumbar are most at risk to develop the degenerative changes of spondylosis.

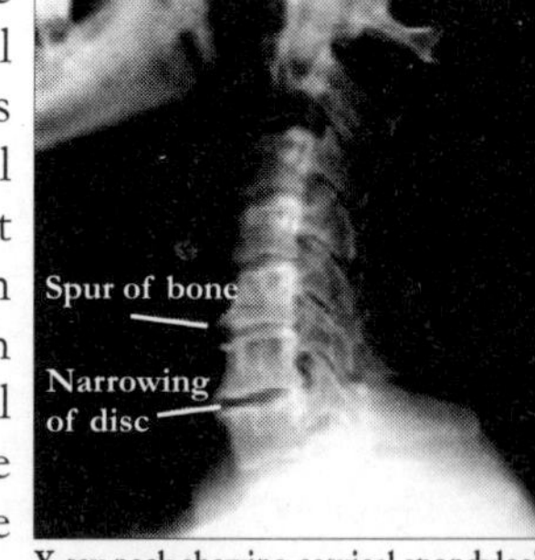

X-ray neck showing cervical spondylosis

Stick to the simple rules

Have you ever carefully watched a professional weightlifter lift a weight? He sits on his haunches close to the weight he is about to lift and without bending his back, picks the weight up from a level close to his chest. He then straightens his knees to stand, and lifts the load up from his chest to take it above his head. During this entire manoeuvre, he keeps the weight as close to the body as possible such that the centre of gravity remains well within the axis of his body. This allows him to lever the load without burdening the spine too much. Just remember this simple principle whenever you decide to lift a large load: one, keep your back straight while picking up the weight; two, keep your back straight; and three, keep the weight as close to the body as possible. This way you will never risk hurting your back.

When age catches on

An old building, an antique car, vintage furniture, and veteran bones, all have something in common. They are all special, and yet, also fragile. The story of intervertebral discs is not much different except that the changes of ageing set in rather early.

While you are still celebrating your youth, and are in your 20s, the jelly-like nucleus of the intervertebral discs begins to lose its elasticity. Its mucopolysaccharide content begins to degenerate. Over the years, this inelasticity of the discs becomes worse. Once they become rigid, their cushioning capacity is lost. At the same time, their outer capsule also develops weak points.

Even a minor bending strain or lifting a small weight can damage them. A cartilage fragment can break off easily from a disc, move into an intervertebral joint and lodge against a ligament, nerve root or a bunch of nerves and cause pain and other symptoms.

While you can't stop yourself from getting older, you can be sensible and avoid activities which might trip your back.

Posture and poise

Physicians and therapists who treat backache often talk about the virtues of good posture. Before we delve into the subject any further, let's understand what posture means. Put simply, it is a position of the body and limbs. We take on different positions for carrying out different activities. Thus, we may sit, stand, lie in bed or walk, hop and run – each time our body and limbs take a different position or a different pose. Even that can have different shades. For

instance, while sitting on your work desk, you sit in a stance quite different from how you may sit while relaxing on a sofa or reclining chair. Likewise, even while you may be standing each time, your stance would be entirely different while talking to your boss, with your partner on a dance floor or if you were waiting for a bus. The point simply is that several factors govern your posture: the situation, your mindset, the furniture you may be using and your personal habit. Clearly, with so many variables, it is not simple to frame any common rules.

Yet, some basic rules do apply:

Mantra 1: Whatever you do, do not strain your back. Keep your back straight, whether you're sitting, standing, lifting, or bending down.

Mantra 2: Pick your furniture well. Use a proper chair, sofa, car seat, computer table, bed and settee, which is suitable to your size and the job at hand.

Mantra 3: Use proper equipment. For instance, if you like gardening, invest in a shovel that you can dig with, without bending your back. Use a trolley for moving the pots. Lifting a heavy pot without your muscles being in shape is a recipe for disaster.

Mantra 4: Start now. The sooner you begin the better it is. Good posture etiquettes are best acquired at a young age. Habits never change easily. This rule applies equally if you are conscious about damage control. Remember, damage to the intervertebral discs often begins early in life. By being careful, you can check this wear and tear.

Mother Nature has designed the human back with considerable forethought. She has kept a huge margin of safety for man to err. Think about it: Can you name any similar man-made structure that can take so much punishment, and still stand proud? The human back simply has no match. Still, since everybody has a penchant for numbers these days, how about this? A normal adult disc can endure a load of up to 545 kg per sq. inch before it gives way. Contrast it with what a vertebra can stand. It is likely to break if the load increases to beyond 450 kg per sq. inch. Clearly, Mother Nature has been more than generous. The idea is to make the most of this benevolence.

PART TWO

Common Back Problems

Back problems have become increasingly common in the modern age. Some 70-90 per cent people experience back pain during their lives. While most improve within a few weeks, 10 per cent suffer from a more severe condition and need frequent help.

Many of the problems are born out of the ills of modern living. This push-button age has reduced the opportunities for physical activity, accelerated the pace of life, and given rise to greater levels of stress. The preference for fast food has also worked against the body and mind. These lifestyle changes conspire to put the

back muscles and ligaments to shame, render the body stiff and inflexible, increase the girth and place an additional burden on an already weak back.

A host of conditions can cause back pain. Back strain and sprain, slipped disc, acute lumbago, sciatica, thinned-out discs, degenerative changes in vertebrae, and narrow spinal canal – all can put you to the sword. Unless managed well and on time, these conditions can turn chronic and mess with the quality of life.

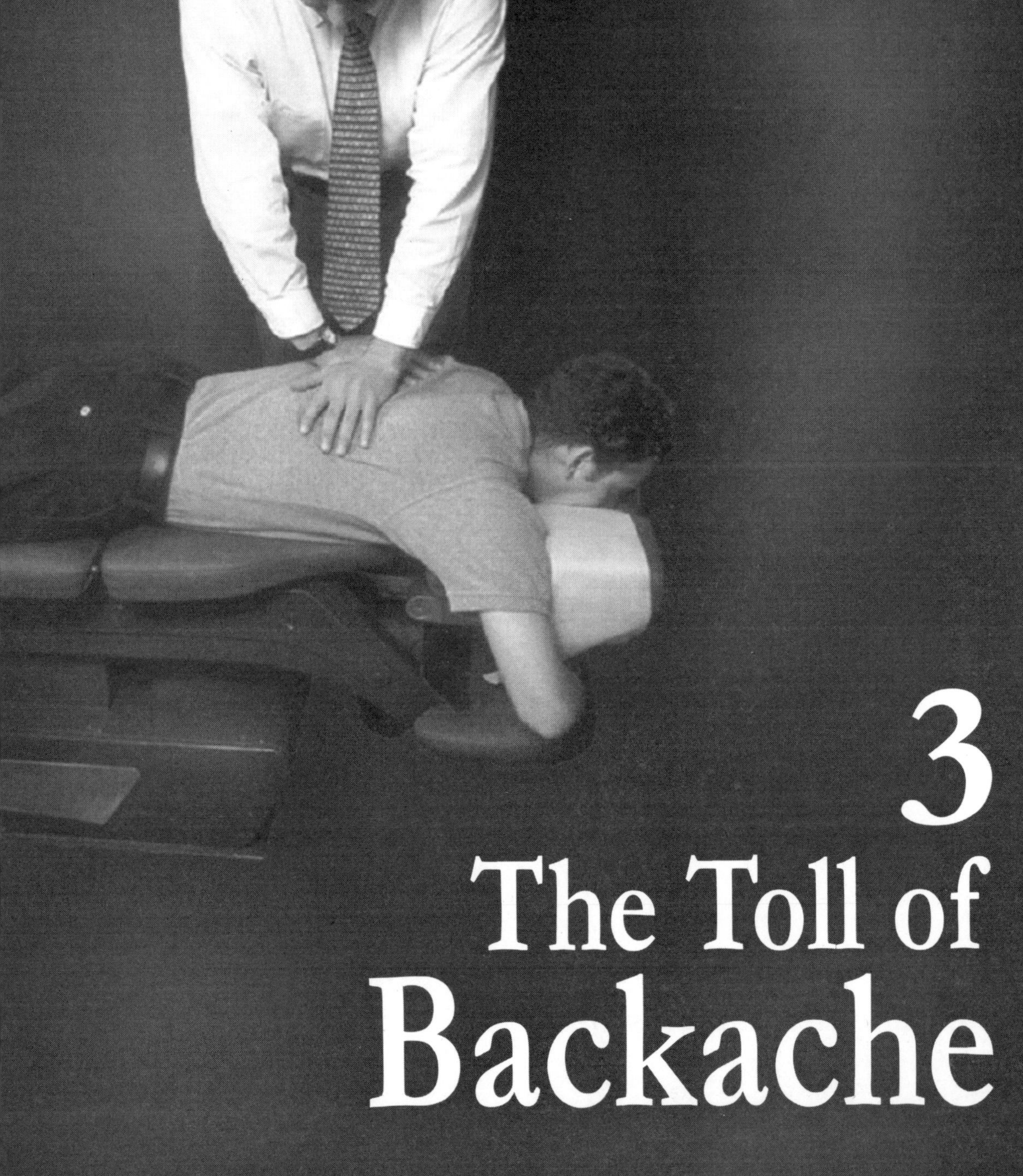

3
The Toll of Backache

Ever since human beings began to stand upright, they have been having trouble with their backs. But today, the epidemic of *bad backs* has become widespread all across the world. Few people go through life unscathed, without suffering the ignominy of their backs being pummelled, pulled, heated and drugged. Quite so, a healthy back is an owner's pride and a neighbour's envy.

Vital statistics

Backache, with the possible exception of common cold, is the most common physical ailment to affect the human race. Different studies on backache reveal different numbers, yet 70-90 per cent of people endure back pain at some period of their lives. Both sexes suffer, and contrary to common belief that backache is an ageing process, trouble usually strikes early. It is the most common cause of time-off-work among the young and middle-aged people who are in their 30s, 40s and 50s. The affliction is pandemic, permeating all nationalities, all social groups, and all professions.

Until not so long ago, the situation was radically different in the Third World. People led more active lives, did more physical work, had a frugal diet consisting of more fibre and less fat, and were trim and fit. The modern-day automation has changed the way of life. Most of the work, travelling, and play are done sitting down. This hypokinetic lifestyle has set back the human back and it has become more vulnerable to damage.

Even though life continues in contrasting styles between villages and cities, the burgeoning numbers of middle class have taken to the new lifestyle. Affluence and automation have hit villages too. Only modalities are different – while the rich may travel in sports utility vehicles and bigger cars, village people have taken to tractor trolleys and makeshift *jugads* and *Marutas*. French fries, chips, burgers, pizzas and the like, jostle with Indian fast food for a quick bite. These major changes in the way of life have led to a marked increase in the number of people suffering from backache.

The experience of the authors is no different. Today, around one-third of all orthopaedic patients who visit us suffer from back problems.

The outcome

Of those affected with backache, 70 per cent suffer repeated attacks. Most of them do well and recover within a span of two months, but suffer flare-ups now and again. However, 5 per cent are less fortunate and go on to develop chronic backache. Studies suggest that at any given time, around one per cent of the population is laid up in bed and off work due to severe back trouble.

Now the good news: most sufferers are relieved of acute back pain within a week. People who don't get well by this time stand a pretty good chance of recovery over the next three weeks. Thc improvement occurs regardless of the treatment taken. True to the saying, time is the best balm. However, around 10 per cent sufferers continue to be in pain and take a month to recover.

All those who take longer to recover must stay on guard: they are likely to suffer repeatedly, more frequently, and enjoy shorter spells of pain-free periods.

The age at which you suffer the first attack also affects the outcome. Those who endure their first attack of backache at a young age are more likely to fall prey to serious back trouble with age. Yet, those

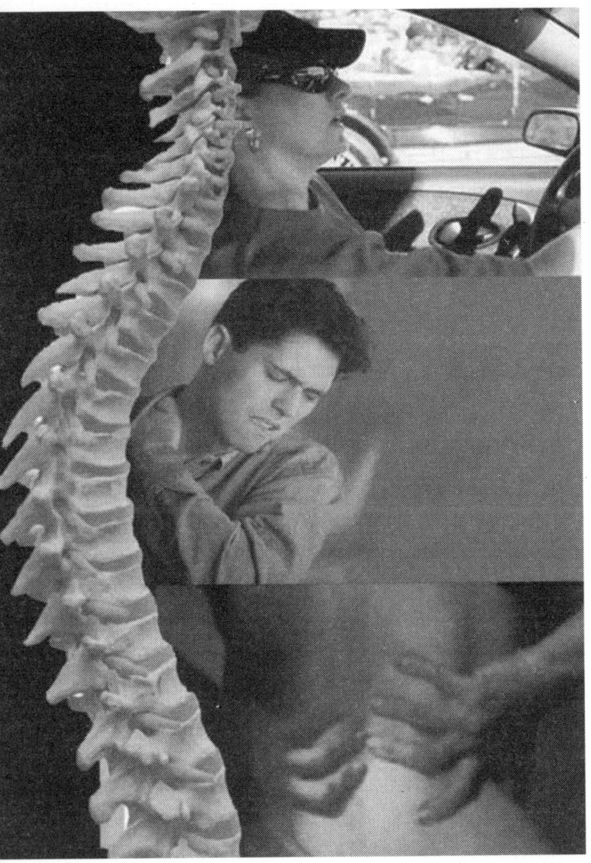

who are young are also likely to recover more quickly since their back is not so run down as in the older people. In contrast, older people generally take longer to recover. They are also more vulnerable to attacks of back pain and may suffer easily if they strain their back lightly.

The economic cost

Backaches cost the sufferer, family, community and the nation considerably by way of lost man-days and productivity. Add to this the cost of medical care, and the family may groan under the burden. Frequent visits to the doctor, expensive tests, physio-therapy, surgery and the psychological ill health may bring the total cost to an astronomical sum. The cost is particularly high for those who suffer from chronic back pain.

Even where the exchequer's money covers the cost of public health care, the expenditure is considerable. We may not have the figures for India, but the annual cost of backache treatment in the United States has been calculated to be $ 75-100 million.

The simplest way to cut down the cost is by solving the problem at an early stage. Nearly 95 per cent of medical cost on back care relates to people with chronic backache.

Backache in specific groups

Women

Young women are particularly at risk to develop back pain during pregnancy. By the time a woman is into the fourth month of pregnancy, her body proportion and weight distribution begins to change. With the pregnant uterus transmitting weight to her lumbar spine, the centre of gravity shifts forward, the natural curvature of the spine becomes exaggerated, and the muscles of the lower back get shortened. This upsets the body balance and gait. While she tries to balance herself by leaning backward slightly at the waist, this shifts the weight to her heels when she walks. As a result, she develops an awkward waddling gait and may suffer acute back pain.

However, if she prepares herself well, she can avert the suffering. Regular antenatal exercises can strengthen her back and abdominal muscles and she can enjoy the rigours of motherhood without causing any damage to her back.

She must also spare time for post-natal exercises once she has given birth. This is the best recipe to check acute backache while nursing your baby.

Young people

Young people possess boundless energy and enthusiasm. Much of their back problems relate to injuries suffered during adventure sports, athletics and contact outdoor games. Often, out of their ebullience they return to full physical activity and active sports before their injury has had a chance to heal.

Some young students also suffer due to poor posture while studying. They slouch over their desk or slip into an unhealthy posture while staying up in bed at night to read. Vigilant parents, grandparents and teachers can check these backbreaking bad habits.

4 Why Backache is so Common

Beep…beep…it's time to wake up, you've to catch a flight – buzzes the palmtop. Rubbing his eyes, Rohan looks at his old faithful, pats it so that it stops relaying the message, and rushes to the bathroom. He has to catch a late-night flight from the Indira Gandhi International Airport for J F Kennedy Airport, spend the next day-and-a-half meeting and discussing new projects with half-a-dozen prospective clients in New York, and be back in office to make a presentation to the company's board members in three days' time. His company is all keyed up for a mega expansion plan, and he must do well to stay high in the reckoning of the bosses.

His wife Sonia is away, doing a night shift at a call centre in Gurgaon. She would be working through the night, attending to the calls that people from Uncle Sam's country make. Sonia will have to be up and attentive to understand their problems and come up with intelligent solutions so that the callers feel happy and satisfied. "It's back-breaking work with little or no respite," she would often tell Rohan, but as she was doing so well, neither she nor Rohan dared to take a decision about her leaving the job.

Just this morning his mother had called from Lucknow, chiding him, "*Beta* (son), both you and Sonia are not getting younger. Isn't it time that the stork visited your home?" She had given a sermon for five minutes, but he did not utter a word. Wasn't she right? Did life also not exist beyond a career and capital?

As he settled down into the cab for the usual 20-minute ride from Vasant Kunj to the airport, Rohan took out his mobile and sent an SMS, "So long, darling. I'm leaving for New York tonight. Shall be back on Saturday. Love you." The last few days had really been tight. They had had no time together.

Life rushes by, a slave of the time. Just like Rohan and Sonia, we stay trapped in life's frenzy, unmindful of its sweetness, beauty and joy. We even forget the basic rules of life, and gradually but surely walk on the path of self-detonation.

The modern order is a conspiracy against life. The jet rush, long hours on laptops, late nights, little time for self, unremitting stress, burning ambition vying with healthier emotions and jettisoning the joys of life – more and more people today are succumbing to the vile ways of modern age, and are getting distanced from the basic plan of life. No more the joys of mingling with Nature, rushing in a field to catch a butterfly, trudging long distances on foot, or carrying out chores that demand high physical fitness.

Man, the unnatural animal, the rebel child of Nature, has come a long way from where he began. Trapped between an endless glut of machines, we cannot think of life without cars and aeroplanes, remote control buttons, cordless and cellular phones, call conferences, net chats, and the like. With little need to move either the body or limb, leading lives of plentiful luxury, too much food and too little exercise, absence of feeling, narrowness of outlook, lack of passion, and feebleness of thought, we are simply burdening our bodies and minds.

The conspirators

The conspirators are many, and each combines with the other to put your body and back to shame.

The couch-potato factor

The modern couch-potato lifestyle gradually wears away the power of your ligaments and muscles, and weakens the bones. As you sit closeted behind one or the other buttons, drifting from one machine to the other, you hardly move a limb or a muscle. Deprived of physical activity and exercise, the ligaments and muscles lose their tone, their flexibility and strength, and become unfit to carry out the functions of the back machine. They get damaged easily and suffer stress and strain when put through simple tests of daily life. The bones also become weak, with osteo- porosis setting in at a faster pace than you would care to accept.

So, stop being a lump on a log, and bowl over the life of inertia. There can be several simple ways, and all you need is a little imagination and attitude. Think, and you may come up with the answers. If you don't, simply turn to page 59 for solutions.

Work-related mechanical strain

Long, continuous hours at work can also strain your back. Jobs that require sitting bent over for hours behind a worktable, laptop and personal computer; criss-crossing between continents on crammed aeroplane seats; lifting suitcases and travel bags; bending and twisting into awkward positions; and whole-body vibrations (such as caused by long-distance driving) expose the elements of your back to considerable mechanical strain.

As a result, while your ligaments and muscles get tired, the intervertebral discs, bones and joints suffer wear and tear, premature changes of ageing and osteoarthritis. The longer time you spend on such a job, the higher is the risk.

No marks for nervous stress

Forcing yourself to meet never-ending deadlines, constant jet setting, bottling up too much nervous anxiety and carrying negativc emotions burdens your body with negative chemistry. As your sympathetic nervous system goes into an overdrive, your adrenal glands release much too extra stress hormones. The adrenaline sparks a riot in the body. You end up having extra tense ligaments and muscles, which fall easy prey to aches and pains. The constant tension also easily tires your muscles out. As a result, the body and the back suffer, and the muscles become stiff.

It may not be possible to change the situation at work, but you can learn to ease out of bad stress. Again, there are several easy formulae, and you can pick them at will without disturbing your work schedule or going nuts. Interested? Turn to page 70.

All work and no sleep

If you work 24 × 7, toiling hard or jumping from one time zone to another and do not find proper time for sleep, you are doing your body and mind a major disservice. It is a perfect formula for a burnout, which nobody can quite compensate for. At the end of the day, you may defeat the very purpose for which you

set out into such a rigorous routine. A half-performing employee, howsoever hardworking he or she may be, only attracts derision and no kudos from the boss.

Work you must, but keep life in a balance. Take a good seven hours' sleep each day, observe a weekly Sabbath, and roll your bag and baggage at least once every six to eight months for a holiday with your family. This recipe will keep your batteries charged, your body purring, and your mind alert and active.

A question of ethics

If you flinch and desert the principles you grew up respecting, it plays on your mind and body. Such compromises for vanity or greed can leave you under tremendous stress, and before long, you find yourself pushed deeper and deeper into a

hole. This misery can put your body, back and mind in great anguish.

If you have such moral issues, talk to your family or friends you trust, and abide with what you find most amenable to your inner self. In any case, remember, regular social interaction with people who're positive towards you is the best cushion for work-related stress and strain. You may not share all the events, but can share and concretise your thoughts, and that's often a big relief.

No refunds for belly worship

If you put on excess weight, you burden your trunk and abdominal muscles, and enfeeble them. The bulge in the middle often leads to poor posture. This excess baggage hollows out the lower spine, burdens the spinal ligaments and muscles, throws the weight of the trunk on the posterior vertebral joints, brings early wear and tear changes in the spine, shrinks the diameter of the openings in the spinal canal and puts pressure on the nerve roots. The net result: overweight people are at a serious risk of developing mechanical stresses, strains and sprains of the back, spondylosis of the bones and joints, and compression of nerve roots with often serious consequences.

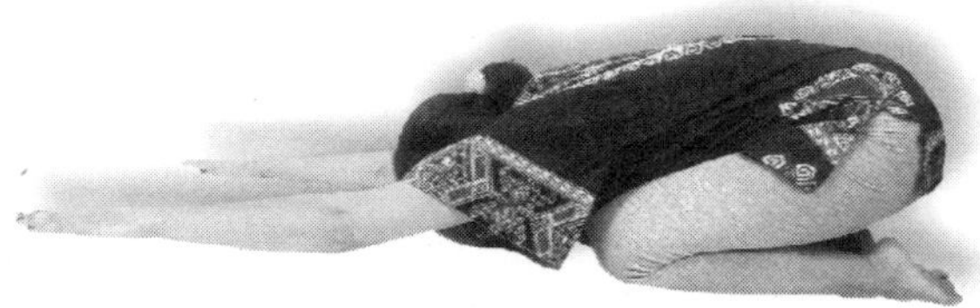

Disregard of body's signals

The human body is blessed with a wonderful system of checks and balances. If the body feels aggrieved, it begins to beep Mayday signals. If you feel a twinge of pain in your back, or find it difficult to bend and move, or your posture has become tilted, think of it as an SOS from the body.

Take active steps to strengthen the back, and none that aggravates the pain. If you do not heed the first signals of body's discomfort, you're liable to walk into bigger difficulties. What may have been remedied initially may soon develop into chronic back trouble.

If you do suffer an acute backache, do not rely on quick-fix measures. Rather, work on a long-term strategy so that the back and the body become healthy and strong.

Lest you feel you are the only one who's facing all the flies in all the ointments in life, think a little more deeply about what Ogden Nash has to say:

Here is a pen and here is a pencil,
here's a typewriter, here's a stencil,
here is a list of today's appointments,
and all the flies in all the ointments,
the daily woes that a man endures
take them, George, they're yours!

5 Common Forms of Backache

Backache can occur due to a variety of reasons – you could strain a muscle, stretch or tear a ligament, suffer a disc prolapse, or be affected by the changes due to advancing age. On a few occasions, the pain may not be related to the back machine at all, and conditions afflicting other bodily systems may be the culprit behind back pain.

This chapter walks you through the common conditions related to the back apparatus. You can find out what transpires when the back suffers a strain or sprain, the intervertebral disc slips out of its place, acute lumbago or sciatica occurs, or the spinal column bears the unhealthy changes of spondylosis. You can also review about spinal stenosis, a condition that results from compression of the spinal canal or the spinal nerve-root exit-points.

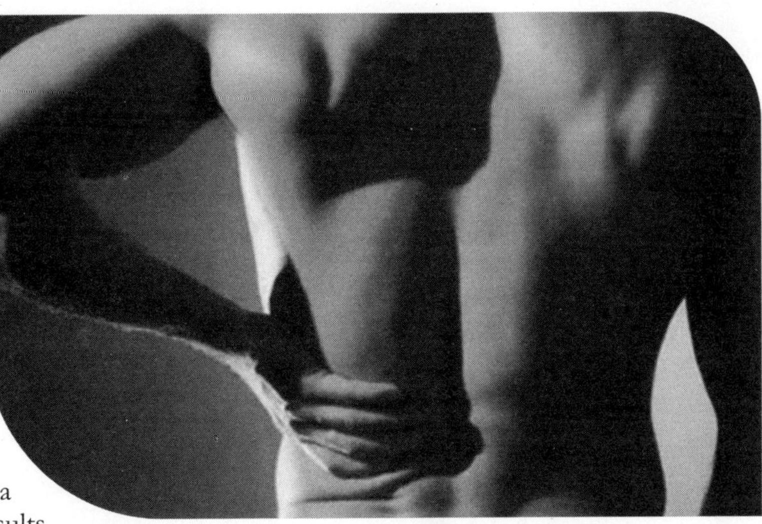

Often, the transition from an acute back strain or sprain to a chronic condition is the result of neglect when things could easily be set right. By being more attentive to treatment and by taking preventive measures in time, you can quickly arrest the damage. If ligaments and muscles are strengthened, flexibility of the back is improved and proper attention is paid to the posture, you could escape being hemmed in by recurrent attacks of backache.

Strains and sprains

Acute strains and sprains of the back are rather common. They may follow such trivial injury that you may not even pick the event, but are often caused by a physical injury, such as during lifting of heavy objects, moving weighty items or carrying out vigorous activities. Sprains can also occur if the back is bent or overextended.

Back strain

You could strain your back muscles in many ways. If you maintain a poor posture, or remain under constant stress, or perform a forceful activity all of a sudden, you are liable to strain them. Once that happens, the muscles respond by going into spasms, and tie up in hard knots that may press upon nerves and excite pain.

Prevention

You can take several measures to avoid straining your back. Keep your muscles strong and supple by exercising them regularly, observe the basic rules about

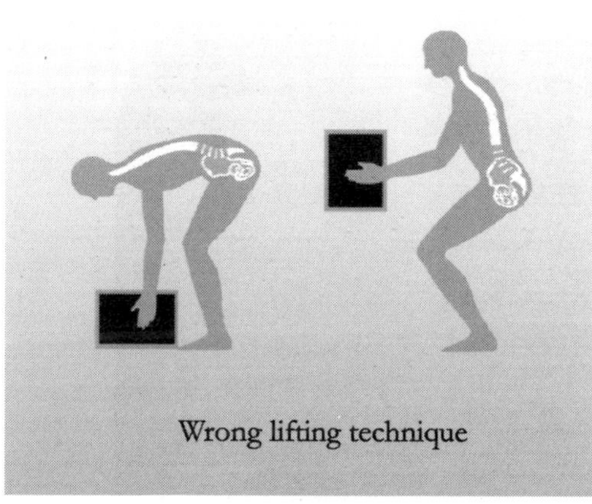

Wrong lifting technique

good posture, and train your mind to stay calm. Do not indulge in any severe physical activity on an impulse. If you decide to weed out your garden, paint your house, or play a game of football with your child, do a proper warm-up before putting yourself on the job.

Treatment

Do not panic, but you must rest in bed. If you're careless, you could easily aggravate the injury. Rest, simple pain-relief pills, muscle relaxants, a hot-water bottle or a heat pad placed against the back should provide relief. If you do not improve within the next 48 hours, consult your doctor.

Back sprain

If you bend or overextend your back, the ligaments of the back can get severely stretched or torn. This is called a sprain.

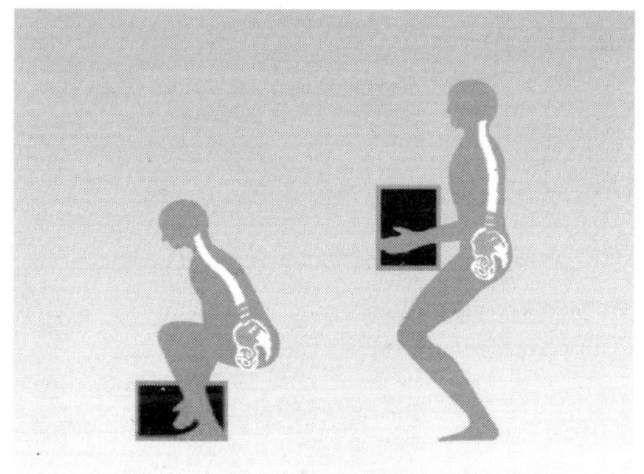

Correct lifting technique

Causes

A back sprain can happen in a number of ways. You could be bending over to pick your shoes, and may suddenly feel a catch of pain in the middle of the back that doesn't let you straighten up. Or you could be travelling in a car, and suffer at the hands of a sudden deceleration. Acute back sprain might also follow a severe fall while running, jumping or climbing.

Treatment

You should rest in bed. If given rest, the stretched or torn tissues get an opportunity to heal. To relieve the pain, you might take painkiller pills every few hours, and apply a heat pad or a hot-water bottle against the back.

Sometimes cold packs also help, particularly over the first 24 or 48 hours. If the pain does not let up within two days, you must see a doctor.

Long-term plan If a ligament gets scarred, it may cause recurrent pain. Once the acute phase gets over, the best solution is to strengthen and tone your back muscles through regular exercise. This will ease the pressure on the ligaments and joints of the back, freeing you of a constant chronic problem.

Disc injuries

The intervertebral discs in the spinal column are pretty well built. They can withstand a sizeable amount of vertical pressure without much difficulty; however, a sudden twisting movement can undo them. For instance, if the vertebrae above and below a disc are suddenly forced to rotate in a reverse direction, the outer casing of the disc can split. In this situation, the thick, gel-like nucleus of the disc bulges or protrudes out. This is known as slipped disc. Frankly, it's a misnomer, since the disc doesn't slip out of its place; only a part of it prolapses or herniates out. Such injuries of the disc are most common in young people aged between 20 and 45 years. A disc prolapses most commonly in the lower back, but a disc may also sometimes bulge or prolapse in the neck, and, rarely, the upper back.

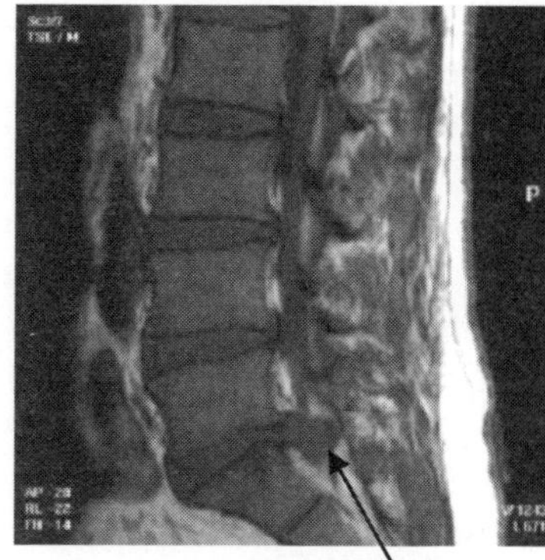

A prolapsed disc

Causes

An acute prolapse usually happens while bending or making a sharp twisting movement. A sudden jerk might also be responsible. You could be lifting a heavy object, and the upper portion of your body might be bent forward.

In other people, the event may not be so dramatic. The disc may prolapse due to simple everyday stress and strain.

Symptoms

Since discs do not carry a nerve supply, they are insensitive to injuries. Neverthe-less, a prolapsed disc is quick to excite symptoms since it bulges and presses against the tissues that run next to it. Often, the ligaments bear the brunt. When a bulging disc stretches the sensitive fibres of a ligament, acute pain is felt at the site of the injury. At the same time, in a protective response, the muscles in the area huddle into a spasm and become stiff.

Sometimes, a prolapsed disc might also press upon a spinal nerve or spinal cord. In that case, the symptoms are acute. Severe pain, tingling, or numbness is felt over the area served by the nerve, and if the affected nerve fibres power the muscles, the affected leg or arm might also become weak.

If a disc prolapses in the lower back and presses upon the tail of the spinal cord, bladder or bowel function may also suffer.

Treatment

If you suspect a disc prolapse and suffer a weakness of limb, bladder or bowel, call your doctor immediately. This requires emergency care. If you don't have any symptoms of nerve involvement, you might wait until later.

A disc that has prolapsed can never return to its intact state again. It will always show, and each subsequent MRI or CT scan will report it. This shouldn't worry you, since the swelling will subside over the next six to eight weeks and the pain will lessen and pass. During this period, your doctor would probably suggest ways to modify your physical activities to avoid further stress on your back. You will also need pain-relief pills. Just as pain becomes less, you may start with physiotherapy. It will lessen the muscle spasm, restore muscle strength and mobility and hasten recovery.

While some people may benefit with traction, others may require an epidural injection or a selective nerve root block to get relief from pain. Those who suffer muscle weakness, loss of bladder or bowel function may require urgent disc surgery.

Acute lumbago

Acute lumbago simply means a sudden intense attack of low back pain. Until the late 19th century, doctors thought the pain to be due to arthritis of the sacro-iliac joint, a condition called sacroiliitis. However, this concept underwent a major revision following the discovery of X-rays. When X-rays of the sacro-iliac joint were taken, they did not show any changes of inflammation or degeneration.

Came the 20th century, and all acute low back pain spreading across the small of the back came to be called acute lumbago. The cause was thought to be a sudden prolapse of the intervertebral disc between the fifth lumbar vertebra and the first piece of sacrum. It now seems likely that slipped disc has also been given too much significance, and it may only be a true cause of the problem in only a small percentage of back-pain patients. This realization has come since the 3-dimensional imaging technology of CT scan and MRI came to the fore. Both methods have improved the visualization of the spine considerably. However, they must still be viewed as tools for problem solving or confirming a suspected clinical diagnosis. They also cost a packet. So, you should only think about undertaking these tests if your doctor feels the necessity for them.

Symptoms

You may have lumbago, if you develop a sudden low back pain that's severe enough to interfere with your daily activity. The pain could have begun subsequent to an unaccustomed physical exercise or excessive strain at work. Often, the pain is so intense that you find difficulty in walking without a slight tilt. While sitting also, you may have difficulty and you may be forced to sit rather awkwardly.

If you look at your weight chart or belt size, you may realize that you have gained weight recently, and have been less active lately.

You don't necessarily have to be old to suffer this condition. In fact, you could be as young as 15 years or as old as 60 or more before your first attack confines you to bed.

Diagnosis

You can help your doctor diagnose your condition by providing him the complete details of your problem and by going through a proper physical examination. A good clinical history and clinical examination are still the best aids to a correct diagnosis in back pain. This also helps the doctor decide the best course of treatment.

Most people do not need spinal X-rays, CT scan or MRI to diagnose their problem. In fact, X-rays and MRI many times confuse the issue rather than solving the problem.

For instance, you may have a few symptoms but your MRI may display disc prolapse at several levels in the spine. Likewise, you may recover completely from pain and still your X-rays may put on view changes of advanced degeneration in the spinal joints. Let this not confuse you, or burden your mind. If you feel unsure, discuss with your doctor.

The basic flaw

Commonly, the problem may relate to weak lower back or abdominal muscles, strained muscles in the thigh or chest, or poor posture. The condition may sometimes be associated with a varying degree of disc injury. Muscle weakness and a long-standing ligament injury may aggravate the damage to the disc.

Treatment

You should rest in bed, take pain-relief measures under your doctor's guidance, and as soon as you can, embark on an active exercise programme. Unless you do so, you're liable to weaken your muscles. A person who remains in bed loses the strength of the muscles at a brisk rate. But if you start simple exercises, you can preserve and gradually build on the muscle strength.

If you let this opportunity slip to make your back stronger and more flexible, you are likely to get entrapped in a vicious cycle of recurrent pain which may develop into chronic changes.

You must also obtain suitable guidance about posture and imbibe healthy habits.

Sciatica

Sciatica is a pain felt in the buttock and which runs down the back of the leg. It occurs when the sciatic nerve or its roots get irritated. Usually, the damage happens at the site where the sciatic nerve leaves the spinal cord, but less commonly, sciatica may also result from an injection given into the buttock that erroneously is too close to the fibres of a sciatic nerve.

Sciatica is rather common. A large number of people suffer at least one episode of pain during their lives. Often, only one leg is affected. In 20 per cent people, sciatica follows an attack of acute low back pain. Some find their back pain disappear miraculously, but it shifts to the leg.

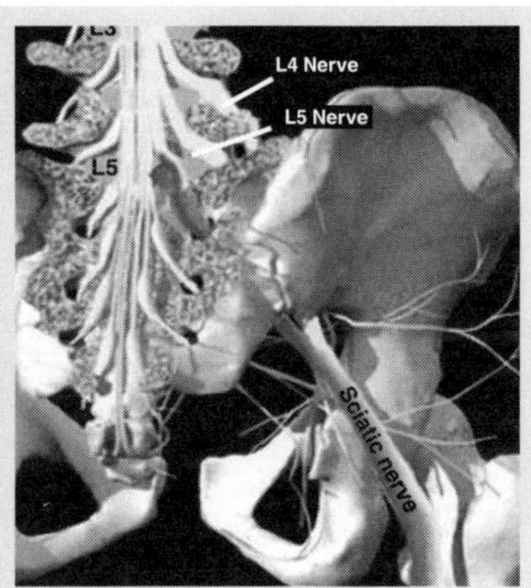

Causes

A herniated disc is the most frequent cause. Most people who suffer sciatica keep poor posture, lead sedentary lives, spend long hours glued to their desks or laptops, live under nervous stress and are obese.

Osteoarthritis of the spine can also be a cause. The bony spurs that appear on the spine might encroach into the nerve roots, and cause sciatica. Rarely, a spinal tumour or a fracture of the spine might compress the nerve roots.

Some women also develop sciatica in the last months of their pregnancy. This occurs due to a shift in the centre of gravity and the changes in posture necessitated by the growing baby.

Symptoms

The classical symptom of sciatica is pain radiating down the leg. The pain may be continuous or spasmodic, and its intensity may vary. While some people feel a dull ache, others suffer from acute shooting pain. In fact, the pain can be so agonizing that you may feel discomfort even as you rest in bed. If you sit on a low chair or bend forward or cough, the pain gets worse.

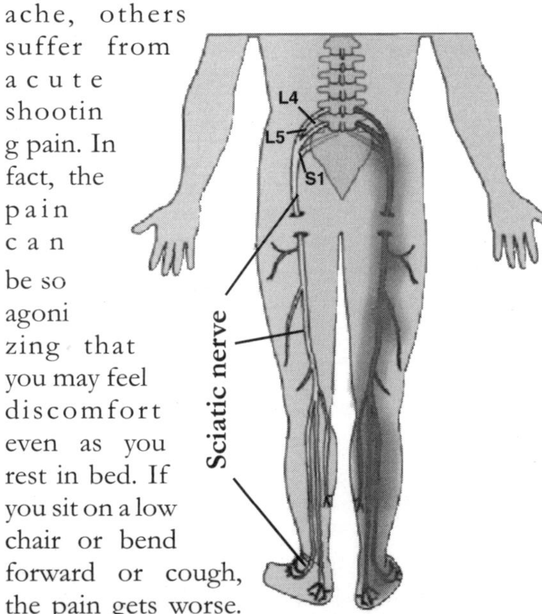

The pinching of nerve roots causes numbness, tingling and burning along the course of the nerve. If the motor fibres of the nerve suffer, you may not be able to move your toes, and could face difficulty in lifting your foot. In severe sciatica, you may find it impossible to stand or walk.

Treatment

You should rest in bed. Lie on your back with knees bent or keep a pillow under the knees. This way you might be able to relieve the pressure from the sciatic nerve and get rid of your symptoms. You will also require pain-relief pills for a few days.

Recovery from sciatica could take several weeks. You would require regular physiotherapy, observance of good posture, exercise, heat treatment and possibly, traction to hasten relief.

Some severe cases involving insufferable pain despite observing complete bed rest or muscle weakness or other nerve deficit or frequent relapses of pain may need surgery.

Spondylosis

Spondylosis is simply the wear and tear of the spine. By the time a person reaches middle age, it is well set in. The degenerative changes affect the vertebrae, the facet joints, and the discs. While the vertebrae suffer excessive growth of bone and develop bony spurs called osteophytes, the facet joints undergo reactive osteoarthritis. The ageing effect thins the cartilages and dries the fluid that lubricates the facet joints, leaving one bone rubbing on another. The intervertebral discs between the vertebrae also shrink, causing the intervertebral spaces to narrow down.

Due to the changes, the nerve roots emerging from the spinal cord suffer pressure symptoms, causing chronic back pain. Since the intervertebral joints also undergo fusion, the mobility of the spine gets restricted.

Above the age of 40, people increasingly suffer from spondylosis. If a person has a malformed spine or has incurred a spinal injury, spondylosis may also

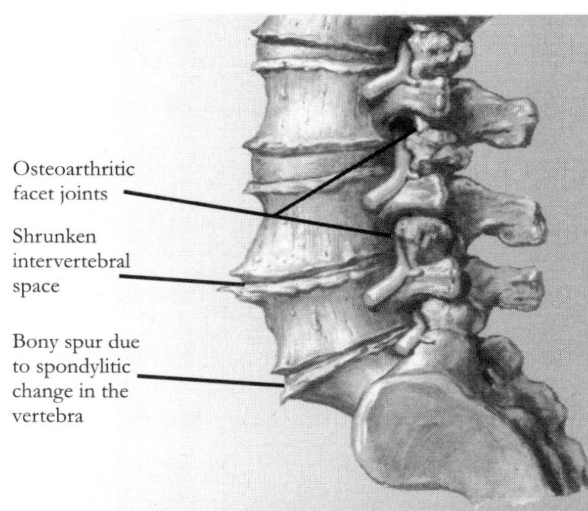

Changes of lumbar spondylosis

occur at a younger age. The condition is more common in men than women due to the more vigorous life men lead.

Spondylosis mostly affects such areas of the spine which are rather mobile and carry much of the body's weight. In the neck, the most mobile segments are the fifth and sixth cervical (C5/C6) and the sixth and seventh cervical vertebrae (C6/C7).

Hence, changes of spondylosis are most marked in this region. The condition is known as cervical spondylosis.

In the lumbar area, the changes are most severe between the fourth and fifth lumbar vertebrae (L4/L5) and the fifth lumbar and the first piece of sacrum (L5/S1) since this part of the spine bears the maximum load due to body weight and the bending forces. These changes causes lumbar spondylosis.

Symptoms

The symptoms can be persistent but more often they are spasmodic and can vary greatly in intensity. The symptoms may include:

- A stiff neck or back with painful and restrictive movements.
- Chronic dull pain in the neck or lower portion of the back.
- Aching or shooting pain that travels from the neck to the shoulder, arm and hand or from the lower back to buttocks, thighs and legs.
- Stretch pain in the arms or legs due to pinching of the corresponding nerve roots.

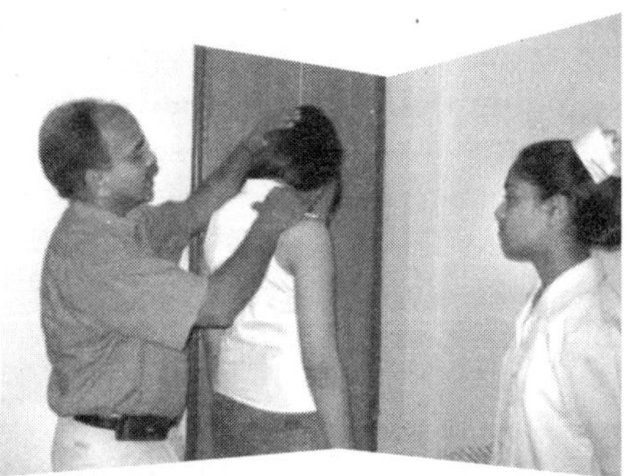

- Numbness, tingling, and weakening in the arm and hand or buttock and leg muscles due to pressure on the nerve roots.

The course spondylosis takes is not predictable. The changes in the spine might not progress or worsen as a person may expect. There may be little deteriora- tion for years, and sometimes the symp- toms may actually become less severe. But it's equally possible that somebody may have pain that persists for months or years together without easing a bit.

Diagnosis

Your doctor should be able to diagnose spondylosis on the basis of symptoms and physical examination. You may be asked to obtain X-rays of the spine. In case of the lumbo-sacral spine, you'll require at least one day's preparation. Your bowel must be cleared with laxatives and gas adsorbent pills. Go on an empty stomach on the day of the X-ray examination so that the bowel does not cast its shadow on the spine. The radiographs (X-ray images) can tell about the extent of the disease, revealing the changes that might have taken place in the vertebrae, facet joints and the intervertebral discs. They cannot however visualize the spinal nerves. Therefore, if the doctor feels necessary, he may ask you to have an MRI or CT scan of the spine.

Treatment

Your doctor may prescribe pain-relief pills. Once the initial pain subsides, the doctor may also suggest some simple exercises to maintain the mobility and increase the strength of the muscles in your neck and back.

The changes cannot be reversed, but that should not be a cause for concern. Do not attach significance to them. The fact is many people with severe changes have few or no problems, whereas those with relatively minor changes may suffer severe pain.

A regular exercise plan to maintain the flexibility and stability of your spine, and reduction in weight to reduce the burden on the back should hold you in good stead. Whenever your symptoms exacerbate, you can obtain relief with pain-relief medications and physiotherapy. Only some people, who do not benefit with these simple measures, might require surgery.

Spinal stenosis

Spinal stenosis is a narrowing down of the canal through which the spinal cord passes. The spinal canal is of a different shape and size in each individual. While in some people the canal is wide and full, in others it is much too narrow. It is this latter group of people who suffer the hardships of spinal stenosis.

Some people also run into difficulty at another anatomical spot. They may suffer from stenosis of the small openings called neural foramina which are situated on the sides of the vertebral column and where the nerve roots emerge from the cord to run down into the legs. A slipped disc or osteoarthritic bony spurs in the vertebral joints can compress the openings and pinch the nerve roots. A slipped vertebra that runs out of alignment can also narrow the spinal canal.

Mostly found in the lumbar region, spinal stenosis can affect people of all ages. Those born with narrow spinal canals suffer at a young age in comparison to those who develop stenosis due to osteoarthritis. The consequence, however, is much the same.

Symptoms

When the central spinal canal is narrow, the person may suffer pain, tingling and numbness in the legs on standing, walking and arching backward. But since the spinal canal diameter widens when a person sits, squats or bends forward, the symptoms may disappear in these postures. If a person is overweight, losing a few kilos may help relieve the symptoms.

If a neural foramen is stenosed, symptoms are different. Since the nerve root is quashed, the person is liable to experience persistent sciatica-like pain.

Treatment

If you experience pain in your back or legs and at the same time feel weak or numb in the limb and/or lose bladder or bowel control, consult your doctor urgently. Your doctor can diagnose the condition on the basis of the clinical history. To confirm the narrowing of the canal, you may be asked to undergo spinal X-rays, CT or MRI scans of the back.

If you develop muscle weakness or lose control over bladder or bowel, you may require urgent surgery. The operation will release the pressure on the spinal cord and limit the damage. Surgery is also generally necessary if you have stenosis of the neural foramen.

PART THREE

Fitness Mantras

The biggest joy in life is perfect health. Yet, no elixir can guarantee you this. The key to this treasure-trove lies in preventive wisdom. A fitness plan that combines regular physical activity, healthy eating and a disciplined routine is fundamental to staying fit and healthy. The sooner you begin, the better it is. If young people could be taught and trained in the virtues of this wisdom at school, backache clinics would soon run out of business.

If positive health calls for finding the time to

strengthen your body machine and paying attention to how you carry yourself, sit, sleep, pull and lift – it also applies to preserving a happier you. A stress-free, wholesome family environment, positive values at home and at work, and spiritual growth may have been sacrificed at the altar of modern living, yet their significance as stabilizing factors in personality development and preservation of good health cannot be overemphasized.

6
Simple Step to
Good Health

If you wish to build a strong and healthy back, you must pay attention to the principles of good health. A fit body and sound mind are the first prerequisites of any healthy back plan. Invest in regular physical activity, healthy eating and a disciplined routine and you may easily fulfil your dream. Just as these are vital *sutras* for body fitness, positive thinking, stress dissipation, and a cheery environment are crucial for a happy state of mind. Unless you are ready for this game plan, you cannot strengthen your back. A piecemeal approach, so common in modern day practice, can simply never work as the health of the back is inseparably linked with the health of the body and mind.

The sooner you set yourself on this path, the better it is. This chapter presents a complete roadmap of perfect health, signposted with all the fundamentals.

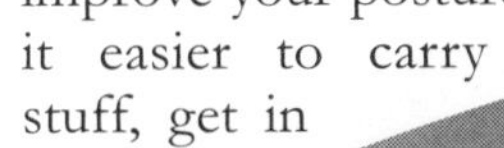

Get moving

Keep moving! That's good advice for almost everyone. The benefits of staying active are immense. A regular exercise programme strengthens the muscles, increases flexibility of the body and helps stabilize your back. If you wake up with your body feeling a bit taut in the morning, exercise helps reduce the stiffness and enhances mobility. It also improves your balance and increases your endurance, while at the same time it helps slow down bone loss that leads to a weakening of the bones which makes them vulnerable to fractures. If that sounds good, there's more. Exercise can also help control your weight, with the result that your back bears much less burden. Regular exercise also helps improve your posture, making it easier to carry stuff, get in and out of the car, and sit, stand and walk with the least strain on the back.

If you remain active, you also reduce the risk of heart disease, high blood pressure and diabetes. A regular exercise programme perks up blood circulation, improves the heart's pumping power, lowers blood pressure and keeps blood sugar under better check.

On top of these plentiful physical benefits, exercise also boosts you psychologically and gives you a renewed sense of well-being. You enhance your mental acuity, concentration and creativity. A balm for the mind, exercise eases stress, negative thoughts and depression.

If these incentives excite you, consider starting now. You have a whole lot of choices, depending on your age, health and fitness.

Get started

Before you get moving, consider the following fundamental issues, so that you extract the maximum benefit out of the exercise routine.

Talk to your doctor

Before you begin with any exercise routine, have a thorough physical examination and discuss your plans with your doctor. This safeguard applies particularly to people over 35 years of age.

Once you get the green signal from your doctor, you can choose any activity you prefer.

Take up activities you enjoy

You should plan on doing activities you enjoy. Broadly, an activity can be of two types: aerobic and anaerobic.

Aerobic simply means with oxygen. All physical activities require a larger supply of oxygen. If the lungs and the circulatory system can meet this demand, and muscles do not feel starved of oxygen, the activity is called aerobic. Such activities are easier on the body and one can benefit from them. Walking, jogging, dancing, cycling, swimming, skating, golfing, badminton and tennis, all fit under this category.

In comparison, anaerobic activities are short bursts of acute physical effort. They rely for energy upon quickfire glucose

metabolism that does not require oxygen. At the end of the cycle, the muscles are flushed with lactic acid. Weightlifting is one such anaerobic activity. Anaerobic activities should only be done by people who have excellent health reserves.

If you enjoy exercising with family members or friends, walking is an excellent activity that allows you the benefit of overall conditioning. It is a simple way to get aerobic exercise, is quite safe, and requires no special gear or training. Just change into a pair of clean cotton socks, proper walking shoes and trunks and set out.

Keep your goals manageable

The frequency and duration of activity are more important than the intensity.

Try to do at least 30 minutes of low to moderately intense physical activity most days of the week. If you have been inactive for a long time, you may tire rapidly at first. So start slowly and gradually try to build up your endurance. Begin by doing 10 minutes a day. Each week, increase this by five minutes, until you start doing 30-45 minutes a day.

Try to find a slot for exercise into your day. But if you're under too much time pressure, do not fret. Although sustained, continuous exercise may give the greatest benefit; you don't need to do all your exercise at one time on such days. Compensate by doing short periods of activity, perhaps in 8- 10-minute periods, that add up to at least 30 minutes.

Be creative

Be imaginative and try and include exercise in your lifestyle. Watch TV or listen to your favourite music while you're on a treadmill. Read a magazine or book while you ride a stationary bicycle. Walking with family or friends can be a way to combine exercise with quality time together. Walking with children provides them with a role model for lifetime habits of healthful activity.

Every move counts

You can boost your exercise total by increasing physical activity in your routine tasks. Use open parking spaces farther away from your destination and walk a little farther. Or walk your way to the local market, post office and other nearby destinations, rather than taking the car out. Use stairs to go to your second- or third-floor office. But consider these activities as a supplement to, not a substitute for, your regular exercises.

The best hour

Exercise whenever it's best for you. Loosen

up with exercises first thing in the morning. Or wait until later, towards the end of the day. Do not exercise right after you eat. Move with a slow, steady rhythm. Take easy, deep breaths, and do not jerk or bounce.

Warm up

Before doing exercise, stir up your body. This could mean doing five minutes of aerobic activity at a low intensity level. Walk leisurely at first or carry out gentle range-of-motion exercises. You may also gently stretch your hamstring muscles. You'll find it helps.

Drink plenty of water

Your body loses fluids when you sweat. Replace The fluids. Water is excellent.

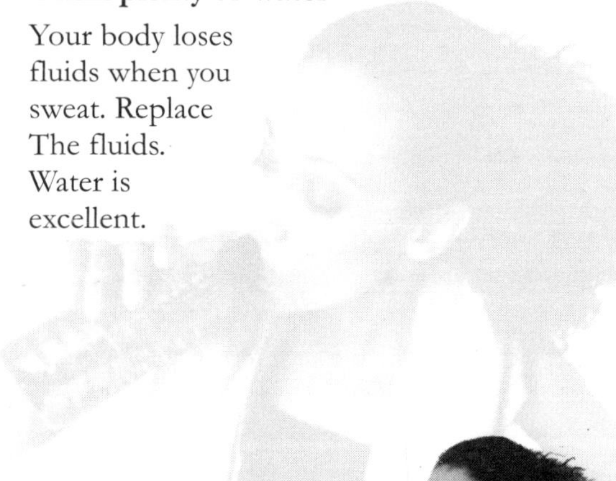

Drink plenty of water before, during and after exercise.

Don't push too hard

If you can't carry on a conversation while you exercise, slow down. You're probably pushing too hard. Let comfort be your guide.

Don't skip

Be careful about skipping exercise. It takes at least two days to come back from the fitness you lose during each day of inactivity.

Listen to your body

Never ignore the body signals that could suggest a health snag. If you feel dizzy, tight in chest, or short of breath, get palpitations or experience pain in chest,
arm or jaw, report to your doctor. Until he or she clears you, take a break from the fitness programme.

Eat well

Eating is not merely for material pleasure; it is the very basis of life. A balanced nutritious diet rich in key vitamins, minerals and other nutrients preserves health, permits us to perform at peak level, and wards off disease. Consider taking the following steps when following a path to good health:

- Eat a variety of foods. It is the best way to insure a well-balanced diet.
- Consume plenty of vegetables, fruits and grain products. They are rich in

vitamins and minerals, high on fibre, low on calorie and fat, and contain natural antioxidants.

- Choose a diet low in fat and cholesterol. As little as one tablespoon of vegetable oil per day fills your need for essential fatty acids. Surplus fat provides excess calories, increases your weight, and accentuates your health risk. Avoid fried and junk foods; restrict butter, cream, *desi ghee*, meat, poultry, fish, and eggs.
- Avoid sweets. They add junk calories, without offering any vitamins and minerals.
- Limit salt intake. Avoid using table salt and eat foods that are salted sparingly.
- If you wish to take alcohol, do so in moderation. Moderate consumption is defined as no more than one drink (30ml) per day for women and not more than two drinks per day for men.
- Eat to live. Take only as many calories as you spend in your daily routine. This will help keep your weight under control.

Plan your meals

A meal plan is simply a guide for eating. It helps you choose the right kind and amount of foods. The first step is to check your weight, do a bit of simple arithmetic, calculate your daily calorie needs, and firm up a diet plan taking the help of a dietician.

Check where you fit

Step on the weighing scale, look up straight, and ask somebody to take the reading. If you know your height, it is easy to know where you stand!

Desirable weights for Indian men and women

Height without shoes (approximate equivalents)			Desirable weight in kilograms (ages 25 and over)	
cm	feet & inches		Men Kg	Women Kg
150.0	4	11	52-56	49-53
152.5	5	0	54-58	51-54
155.0	5	1	55-59	52-55
157.5	5	2	56-60	53-57
160.0	5	3	58-62	54-59
162.5	5	4	59-64	56-60
165.0	5	5	61-65	58-61
167.5	5	6	62-67	59-64
170.0	5	7	64-69	61-65
172.5	5	8	66-71	62-67
175.0	5	9	68-73	64-68
177.5	5	10	69-74	66-70
180.0	5	11	71-76	67-72
182.5	6	0	73-78	69-74
185.0	6	1	75-81	71-76
187.5	6	2	78-83	74-79

Calculate your daily calorie needs

The daily energy requirement of any individual is guided by the physical activity, body weight and health status. The calculation is simple. First, pick the calorie factor that's applicable to you by briefly studying the following table:

Daily calorie requirement per kilogram body weight		
Weight group	**Lifestyle you lead**	
	Deskbound	Moderately active
Overweight	25	30
Normal	30	35
Underweight	35	40

Once you pick up the calorie factor, multiply it by your weight (in kg). For instance, let us consider the calorie needs of a person who weighs 60 kg, has a normal weight and leads a sedentary life. Calculating his daily calorie needs is simple. Just multiply 60 by the calorie factor 30; he requires 1,800 calories a day.

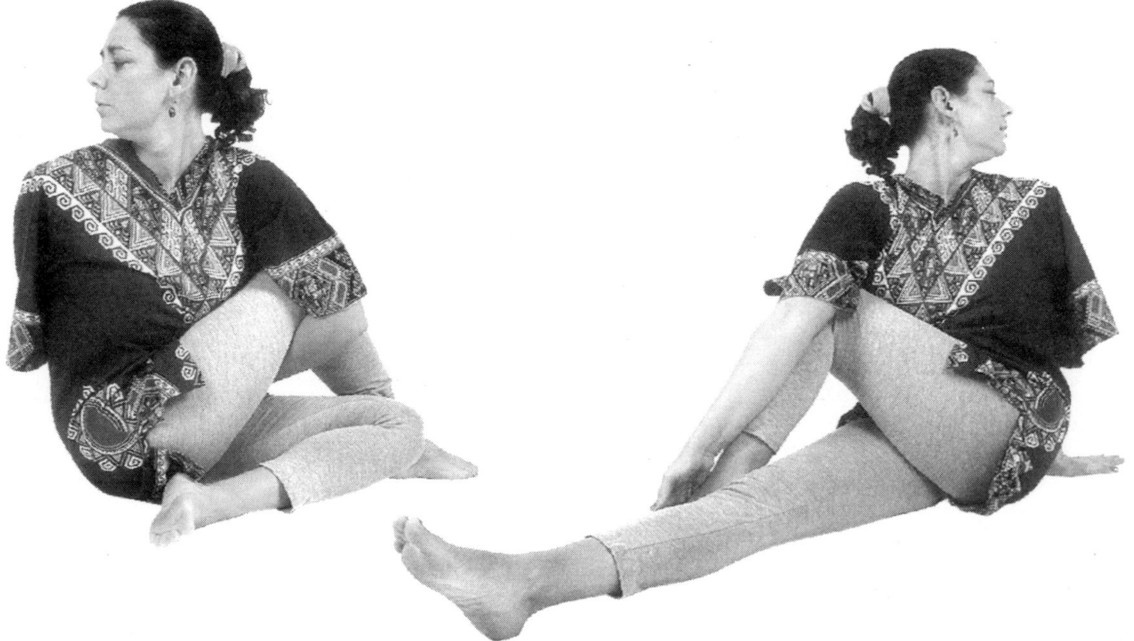

Follow the food guide pyramid

The next simple step is to follow the 'food guide pyramid'. The pyramid is built on sound, healthy diet fundamentals. The plan offers a balance of all nutrients, is high in fibre, rich in vitamins and minerals, and restricts high-fat foods. The arrangement of the food groups in a pyramid emphasizes the kinds of foods you can eat more liberally and those you should limit. While those at the base are healthier foods, those at the apex are best taken sparingly.

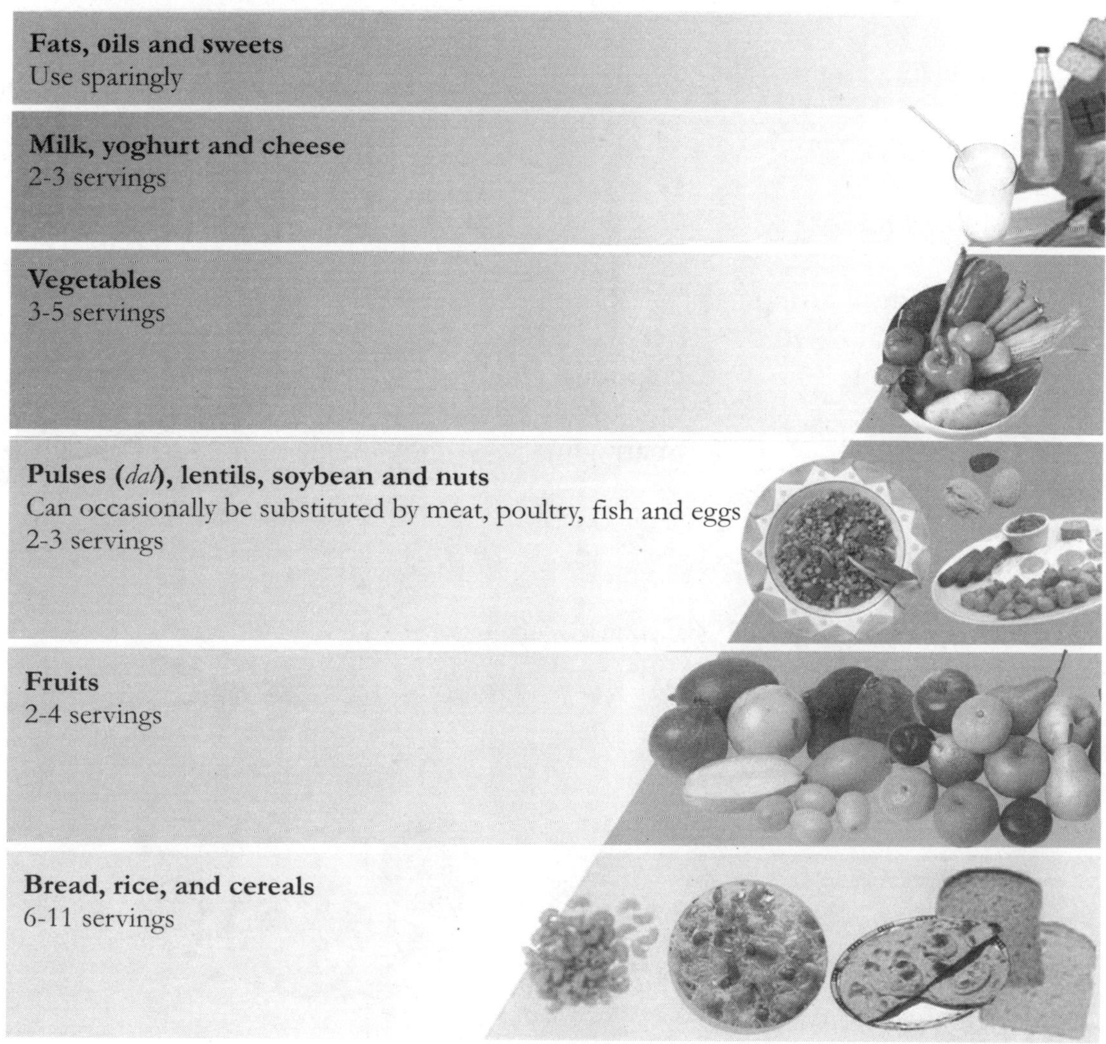

How many servings do you need each day?

Calorie level	1,600 calories	2,200 calories	2,800 calories
Bread group	6	9	11
Vegetable group	3	4	5
Fruit group	2	3	4
Milk group	2-3	2-3	2-3
Pulses/meat group	2	2	3
Fats and oils	2 spoons	3 spoons	3 spoons
Sweets	Sparingly	Sparingly	Occasionally

Sizing up a serving

Here are some examples of what counts as one serving:

Bread, rice and cereals

One *chappati (roti)* made of wheat flour

½ cup cooked rice

One slice whole-wheat bread

One plain *dosa*

¾ cup ready-to-eat cereal

One *kulcha*

25-gram noodles

Vegetables

1-cup raw, leafy green vegetables
½ cup cooked vegetables

Milk products

1 cup low-fat or fat-free milk
1 cup low-fat or fat-free yoghurt
45-gram low-fat *paneer* or cottage cheese

Pulses (*dal*), lentils and soybean

½ cup cooked beans, dried peas or lentils

Fruits

One apple
One guava
One pear
One banana
Two oranges
12 grapes
½ cup 100 per cent fruit juice

Non-vegetarian foods

One egg
45-gram meat
85-gram poultry
100-gram fish

Learn to dissipate stress

Stress is a part and parcel of modern-day life. You can fight it and fail, or you may, instead, learn to flow with it. People who practise the art of living simply aim at training their thoughts and actions and being in control of themselves. A cheery mindset, perseverance and self-belief are the first prerequisites to overcome stress, but the game plan also includes developing a positive social support group, using appropriate behavioural and mental techniques to relax, and turning to time-tested formulae of proper sleep, regular dose of humour, and recreation to dissipate stress. Want to know more, here's how:

Accentuate the positive

A positive mental and emotional approach towards life situations can help you cope with stress. You have just got to believe in your self and hold that you can control much of

all that happens to you. Researchers have found that people who hold a positive attitude about their abilities do not get easily frustrated, remain optimistic, and persevere. They tend to cope well with stress. On the other hand, negative personality traits, such as low self-esteem and an outlook of gloom and negativity can trip people even if they have everything working in their favour. Bolster your psychological defence by equipping yourself with the following mental strategies:

Think positive

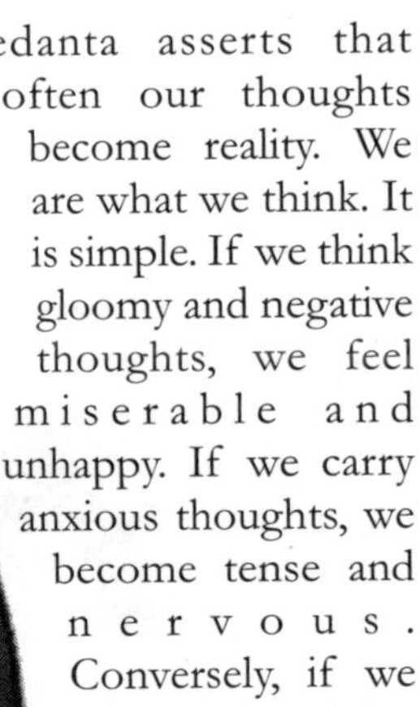

Vedanta asserts that often our thoughts become reality. We are what we think. It is simple. If we think gloomy and negative thoughts, we feel miserable and unhappy. If we carry anxious thoughts, we become tense and nervous. Conversely, if we think healthy thoughts, we feel happy. A positive self-talk that focuses on our capabilities and inner strengths eases stress, while a negative self-talk can push back even geniuses.

Set realistic goals

Setting our goals unrealistically high invites failure. Take a reality check. Assess your strengths, abilities and resources before deciding on your targets and goals. Think big, but be pragmatic. Overstepping your limits can only lead to disappointment, frustration and stress.

Prepare adequately

Plan your work in a step-by-step manner. Specify your target and work out all the details. Rehearse in your mind what the job will require of you. Then divide the target into small accomplishable tasks. While finalizing the plan, also keep allowance for some extra time and expense. Events beyond your control will happen and jeopardise your planning, and if you account for them, it is easy on the nerves.

Prioritize

Decide your priorities and first concentrate on what's most significant to you. If you have more jobs than you can tackle, that's the best way of going about it. Relegate the other jobs to your colleagues, and only carry on your plate what you can chew.

A polite regret works better

A polite 'no' is much better than failing to deliver later. If you have too many jobs on your hands, do not multiply your stress by accepting another. It is wrong to think that if you are honest and refuse, the other person will feel upset.

Abandon wishy-washy attitude

People use two broad types of coping behaviours to triumph over stress: problem-focused coping and emotion-focused coping. The goal of both is to control the stress level. In problem-focused coping, people try to short-circuit negative emotions by taking some action to modify, avoid, or minimize the threatening situation. They adapt themselves to deal with the stressful situation. In emotion-focused coping, people try to moderate or eliminate unpleasant emotions through mechanisms that may not be ideal. For example, faced with a difficult situation you might prepare yourself and deal with it or conversely, indulge in wishful thinking and deny the situation. Both approaches may ease your immediate stress, but relief is temporary if you adopt the latter strategy.

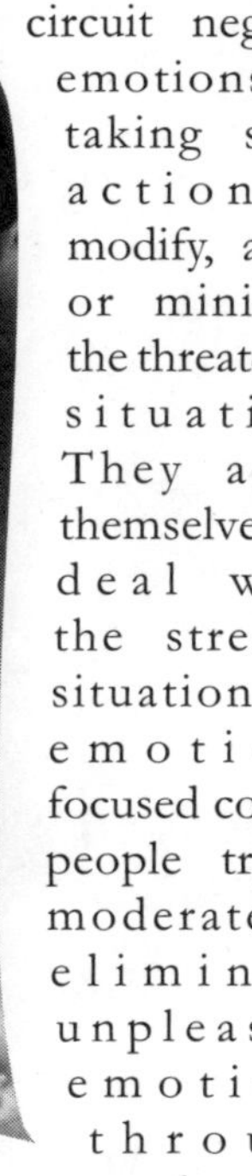

Dissipate your anger healthily

If you experience anger, it needs to be expressed, but carefully. Count to 10, compose yourself and respond in an effective manner. Give the provoker the benefit of doubt, and if you still feel aggrieved, make it known without attacking the other person. Let him know about your disagreement with tact and positive communication skills.

Also, consider learning the art of forgiving. It has a significant positive psychological value. It makes your inner self glow, lowers your blood pressure and heart rate, and your breathing calms down.

Develop a social support system

Discuss your concerns with a trusted friend or family member. Talking help relievcs stress and puts things in proper perspective; it may also lead to a healthy plan of action.

A positive social support system provides emotional sustenance, tangible resources and aid, and information when needed. It makes us feel cared about and valued by others and we also have a sense of belonging that can come in handy during moments of despair. Many large

community surveys have linked social support to good health and a superior ability to cope with stress. In general, people with extensive social ties live longer and healthier than those with few close social contacts. Even the perception of social support can help people cope with stress. Studies have found that the promise of availability of social support by itself mitigates the stressors, irrespective of the actual support received in need.

Even a pet at home can help lower the stress. The companionship acts as a balm to your bruised mind. Studies have found that in times of stress, people with pets made fewer visits to the doctor than those without pets.

Learn to relax

Techniques such as meditation, yoga, muscle relaxation, guided imagery, and slow breathing can help you relax. Your goal is to reduce muscle tension, and lower heart rate, blood pressure and breathing rate.

Turn to time-tested formulae

You could try several age-old simple recipes to knock off the tensions of life. Regular doses of humour, adequate sleep, recreation and sports, soaking in a warm tub, massage, and timely vacation can treat anxiety and stress.

Add laughter to life

A chuckle a day keeps the doctor away. This philosophy has been the basis of therapeutic powers of *hasya yoga* or laughter therapy. A good laugh relaxes the body and mind, eases stress and improves circulation and breathing. Modern researchers investigating into the healing powers of laughter have found that humour also activates the natural stress-relieving chemicals in the brain and improves the defence system of the body. So, it may be a good idea to keep a collection of amusing

books, comics and videos at your bedside and take a regular dose of humour before going to sleep.

Sleep well

Sleep is a wonderful rejuvenator. It refreshes both the body and mind, resolves emotional conflicts, helps to think clearly, and promotes positive mental health. Take regular six to seven hours of sleep during the night and, if possible, a short post-lunch power nap. Indulging in frequent late nights and then cutting on sleep hours are a sure path to court stress.

Some people just cannot get sound sleep. The best way out is to maintain a regular sleep routine.

Switch off the television and PC at least one hour before

bedtime. Light relaxing music, a bath, pleasant conversation and a gentle massage are some sure recipes to keep away from sleeping tablets.

Do not indulge in self-abuse

Alcohol, cigarettes, and cups and cups of caffeine are not the solution to stress. Such substances only mask the problem and can make the situation worse. Their abuse stresses the body and the mind.

Water is a good energizer

Swallow plenty of water every day. Nearly 70 per cent of the human body is water. If opportunity presents, also splash in water. A soak in the bathtub can wipe you clean of fatigue. A good swim, Jacuzzi, or sauna bath makes an excellent remedy for stress.

Massage is good

Touch is a newborn's first contact with the world. As babies, we all snuggle up to our mothers for warmth, comfort and security. A warm rub by a loved one can bring back the same sense of comfort and care to your world.

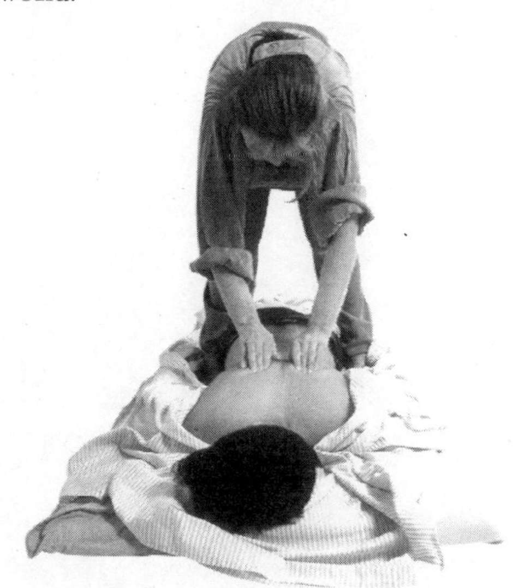

Even an impersonal massage by a masseur has many virtues. It releases tension from aching muscles, stimulates blood flow, eases the mind and body, and fosters a sense of well-being.

Take out time for relaxation

Even though satisfying work is a great tonic, taking time out for recreation is also a must. You can do anything that you like. Read a book, play a game of chess, bridge, carrom, or rummy, or take your family out for a picnic. Going for Nature walks,

enjoying a movie or play, visiting an art gallery, or partying with friends and family – all can help in a big way. Even helping your child do a school project or cooking a dish in the kitchen may work out to be an excellent rejuvenator.

Listen to music

Good enjoyable music is a wonderful remedy to overcome stress and fatigue. Tune in and soothe your self.

Take a vacation

A relaxing, fun-filled holiday is a perfect recipe for good health. It casts a magic effect on your physiological and psychological health and is one sure way to recharge your batteries, cleanse your mind and body and humour your soul. The best way is to simply rest and relax. Remember, the word 'vacation' is coined from vacate, which means 'to leave' or 'go away'. Go away you must – not just physically, but mentally as well. A sedentary desk-bound person may wish to go out and stretch his muscles a bit, but a physically active worker may wish to take a quiet vacation. Let the vacation be a complete change from the routine.

Invest in family values and virtues

If you have strong family ties, a happy family environment and a healthy childhood, you develop a well-groomed personality and can withstand the stresses and strains of daily life without facing a health breakdown. Much of modern-day physical stress has arisen due to changes in the social structure and demise of the age-old joint family system.

A large family may have its difficulties, but it offers a far better emotional, cultural, spiritual and physical support system for each family member. This may seem a bit old-fashioned, but consider the values and virtues that you inherit, and the discipline that's inculcated when you live with the elders, and you may quickly realize the benefits.

7 Sutras to Protect Your Back

If you wish to preserve the health of your back, you should put your heart and soul into grasping the basics of back care. Perfect your posture, stick to the brass tacks of how to perform physical tasks safely and optimise the furniture pieces you use, and you may soon have a back you can be proud of. Most back pains simply occur because people do not follow the ground rules. Often, the abuse is born out of poor habits picked in early years of life, or plain and ordinary sloppiness.

Lest you think that's not the case, how about taking a simple test? Keep a score while we take you through the back-care basics.

The basics of good posture

Good posture is all about carrying the body in its natural elegance without breaking the synergy of the limbs, back and neck. To break bad postural habits, you should be constantly aware of the way in which you sit, stand, move, and sleep. The idea is to carry out all your everyday activities comfortably, with minimal strain on your spine and back muscles.

Sit right

Strange though it may seem, but the human back takes much more strain when a person is sitting rather than standing. The reason is simple. When you sit down, your entire body weight falls on your back. The body dynamics also change. Ordinarily, if you're standing, your back bears and distributes the pressure of body weight quite evenly. Since the spine gets bent in the sitting position, this fine balance gets disturbed. Body dynamic studies make out that sitting without a support subjects the lower back discs to at least 40 per cent higher strain than in the standing posture.

You must, therefore, be very careful

about the strain on the back, especially if you sit continuously for a long stretch of time. Some simple safeguards can help keep the back in good order.

Working on your desk

While working on your desk, take the following measures so that you do not tire your back:

Pull up the chair: Keep your chair up as close to the desk as possible. This way you're less likely to lean forward while working. If you lean forward for much too long, your lower back, shoulders and neck can go sore.

Do not slouch : If you must lean, bend from the hips instead of bending the back. Use an adjustable inclined tabletop to hold the

papers so that you don't tilt your neck in order to read or write.

Sit squarely : Sit on both the hips distributing your weight evenly. If you sit with a tilt, the distribution of weight goes haywire.

Do not twist your trunk : While on the desk, you must always directly face forward. Do not twist or turn your trunk. When you need to turn, move your trunk, hips, legs and feet all as one single unit. This way you're less likely to strain your back.

Use a footrest : Keep your feet propped up on a small footrest. This way the pressure on the lower back shall reduce.

Move about : Change your position often, and do not sit cramped in one place. And after each hour, step out of the chair and walk around. This shall help ease the stress on your back.

Working on a desktop computer

Computers have become an essential part of life. If your work requires you to put long hours on a desktop, take a few safety measures.

Place the monitor and the keyboard at a proper height. The monitor screen should be positioned 15 degrees lower than the height of your eyes and at least about an arm's length away. In the seated position,

your keyboard and work surface should be at elbow height. Sit comfortably upright. Use a proper work chair. Avoid slouching.

If you do a lot of word processing, consider getting a stand to hold documents. Placed adjacent and at the same height to the screen, the stand will limit strain on the neck. You will not need to look up and down repeatedly.

If you use eyeglasses, consider getting a bigger screen so that you can see more clearly without having to poke your chin forward. Do not use bifocal lenses.

Take 30-second micro-breaks every 30 minutes. Move the neck from side to side and turn your back from left to right. This will help prevent the strain on your neck and back.

Reading in bed or chair

While reading, most people, young students included, often tend to slide down a bed or chair. This causes a bend in the mid-back. That's not healthy. If you lie down on a sofa to read with your head resting on the armrest or a doubled up pillow, you shall equally be doing your neck a disservice. It will be angled acutely forward and shall be an easy prey to a strain.

The best posture to read is to sit upright in a chair, but if you like to read in bed, keep a cushion behind the seat of the back and sit up straight. Shift your position frequently. Get up and walk every hour.

Stretch yourself

A big lion-sized yawn or simple stretches are a wonderful natural rejuvenator in the body's system of posture maintenance. If you spend long hours sitting at the same place, carry out these easy stretches:

Close your neck on the shoulder: Sit upright, with your back well supported. Keep your face straight forwards. While still in this position, tilt the neck slowly towards your left shoulder so as the left ear approaches the shoulder. Use your left hand to push and stretch the neck. Hold for five seconds. Return to the neutral position. Relax. Now, repeat the manoeuvre on the other side. Perform this simple neck stretch four times.

Touch down your chin on the shoulder: Sit upright, with your back well supported. Turn the neck towards your left shoulder

and try to touch down your chin on your left shoulder. If you feel comfortable, you can extend the stretch a little. Pull the left shoulder down with your right hand, while you push the chin up with the left hand. Hold for five seconds. Return to the neutral position. Relax. Now, repeat the manoeuvre on the other side. Perform this simple neck stretch four times.

Watching a television

While watching television, it is best to sit up straight in a chair positioned in front of the screen. Also, place the television at the eye level. If you do so, you can keep your head in neutral position while watching. A

television that's kept too high or too low strains the neck. You tend to crane your neck to see the picture, and may end up with a neck strain.

Some people, however, like to lie in bed, or on their side with their head on the armrest of the sofa to watch the television. It is a habit you should never pick. By doing so, you're liable to strain the neck. If you're very tired and feel relaxed using this position, try to keep your neck in a neutral position by sitting up a bit and supporting your neck with cushions.

Talking on the phone

More people than you notice use their necks to cradle the phone so that they may use both their hands for another activity. That's simply not done. It strains the neck badly. If you spend too much time on the phone, consider using a speakerphone or headset, but don't use the neck to hold the phone.

Relaxing on a sofa

While you're relaxing on a sofa or an armchair, sit upright, let the small of your back be fully supported and keep your feet on the floor.

As many people do, don't just slide into a lounging position. That's not correct. When you slide down the chair, your back suffers excessive rounding, and this puts additional strain on your back.

Driving a car

Never slouch

Sit up straight

While driving a car, try to sit upright. Do not grip the wheel too tightly. Keep your head up and try not to hunch your shoulders. Most modern- day cars are equipped with adjustable seats. You should angle your seat backwards a little to support your spine, and position the seat so that you can reach the hand and foot controls easily. If the seat does not provide adequate lumbar support, use a cushion. Always settle down into a comfortable position before driving out.

If you're on a long trans-city drive, stop and stretch every two hours. This will help ease the strain on back muscles and hamstrings.

On a long air flight

If you're a frequent traveller and spend much time shifting from one continent to the other, you should take a few tips. You can get around uncomfortable standard class seats by placing a cushion at the small of your back. This will provide excellent lumbar support. Also, get up every one hour and go for a walk. It will help improve

the circulation and ease the pressure on the back.

Stand easy

In the normal course, when you're standing upright, try and put your weight evenly on both feet. Hold your head up and shoulders back, allowing your lower spine to curve in naturally. You can check if you're doing this right. Stand upright, your heels next to a wall, resting your buttocks, back and head on the wall. If you can fit your arm between your lower back and the wall, you're doing okay. You should also balance your body over its centre of gravity, which is in the pelvis and lower spine. Observ e and note your body posture as you stand before a fulllength mirror. Your ear should be in line with your instep.

If you have to stand for a longer time, you can alternately relax the legs by keeping one leg on the ground, and the other leg slightly raised (with the knee bent) on a footrest, ledge, stone or a railing. Change position frequently. You may also consider taking the

Walk gracefully

Step right. Strike the right posture as you walk. While a perfect walk can enhance your physical appeal, a faulty gait can strain your back and make you look very ordinary. At the fashion schools, they tell you to balance a book on the top of your head and walk. That forces your body into a proper alignment and that is the foundation of both good posture and an attractive walk.

Here's how your body should shape up when the alignment is correct: Rib cage vertical, not tilted forward or backward; pelvis straight (if you had a tail, it would hang straight down, not tucked under between your legs); knees and feet pointing straight ahead.

Stand before a full-length mirror and check yourself out. Hang a plumb line down just in front of your earlobe, and see. The plumb line should fall just in front of the anklebone, just behind the kneecap, through the centre of the hip joint and middle of waist, shoulder, and earlobe.

You must also keep your balance well. The body's weight should be so distributed that the weight does not fall on heels, but on the inner margin ball of the foot, just behind the big toe. Place your feet in a parallel position, tighten the buttocks and inner thigh muscles, lower the shoulder blades and stretch the spine, pulling your head back and up. There! That's a balanced standing position. Now, relax a bit, and start walking slowly. Swing legs from the hip socket and keep your body aligned: Shoulders level, head up and back, shoulder blades lowered, rib cage vertical. With each step, your heel hits the ground first, then the weight instantly rolls forward along the outside edge of foot onto the big toe with which you push off for the next step. This shift of weight is done smoothly, in a continuous, fluid motion. Happy walking. You're looking wonderful.

Use proper footwear

Your footwear has a direct bearing on how you walk and stand. If you care about your back, buy footwear that's well cushioned, with heels no more than 2.5 cm (1 in). High-heeled shoes hollow the lower back, push the whole body out of alignment and also strain the leg muscles.

It is best to wear shoes with laces. Slip-ons have their benefits, but they often make you curl your toes. This transmits tension through the legs and into the back.

Sleep well

The best sleeping position for the lower back is to sleep on one side. Let the legs be drawn up slightly

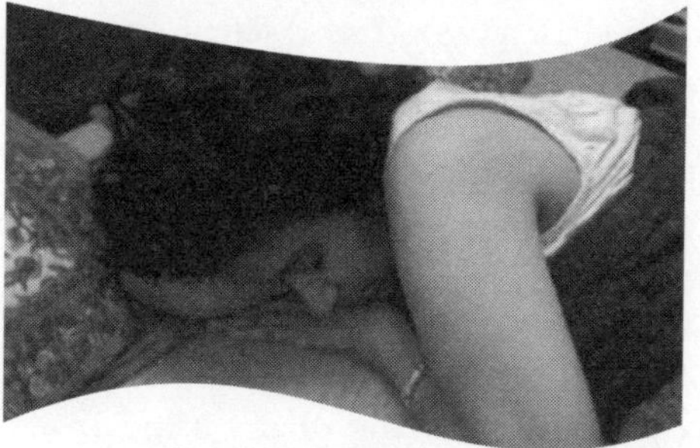

towards the chest.

Now, place a pillow between the legs. If you sleep in this position, you do not risk stretching your vertebral column.

However, if you prefer to sleep on your back, you could do so. It is the next best alternative. If you feel discomfort in the lower back, place a pillow under your knees. It will help ease the strain caused by the pull of the hip flexors and hamstrings.

Some people prefer to sleep on the stomach. This is a far from ideal posture to sleep in, but if it's your favourite, place a pillow underneath your stomach. This will prevent excessive hollowing of the spine. This position also puts some strain on the neck since it is forced to turn to one side.

Performing physical tasks safely

Lifting and carrying objects

When lifting, pushing, or pulling a heavy object, keep the object close to you so that you can use your full strength to move it. To lift an object, hold the bottom edge so that you support the full weight of the object and keep your body balanced as you lift to avoid straining your spine. Keep your back straight and lean forward slightly. Stand up in a single, smooth movement, pushing yourself up with your leg muscles and keeping the object close to you.

Once you are upright, keep the weight close to your body. Keep your back straight and head up, so that your body is balanced over its centre of gravity. Carry the load close to your body. Avoid turning or twisting.

Carting travel bags

If you travel light and just use a shoulder-bag, there is a simple rule. Switch the bag regularly from one shoulder to the other to equalize the strain on your spine and upper back. Heavy shoulder bags carried for any length of time on one side of the body or with the strap around the neck can strain the back.

If you're carrying a single large suitcase, buy one with stable wheels or use a luggage trolley to lug it around. Make sure that the bag is not so big that you have to bend your arms to keep the bottom from bumping on the ground.

Never pack a travel case with too much weight.

That's almost guaranteed to cause back trouble. Rather, divide your luggage into two small bags.

Basics of friendly furniture

It always pays to invest in back-friendly pieces of furniture. That's an indispensable prerequisite to maintenance of good posture.

Sofas and easy chairs

When buying a sofa or easy chairs make sure the seat is not too low or too deep, they are not too soft, and the backrest is not short. If the seat is extra deep, it forces you to either sit forward with your feet on the floor, a position that encourages you to hunch, or with your lumbar region against the backrest and your feet off the floor. Both these positions can trigger back pain. If the seat is too soft or excessively low, then also you are likely to sit in a position that strains the back.

A well-designed back-friendly sofa or easy chair allows you to sit with your lower back firmly against the backrest and rest both feet flat on the floor. The backrest should also be shaped to provide some extra support to the lower back. If it is not, place a cushion or two behind the small of your back.

Work-chair

You must never cut corners while ordering your work-chair. A good work-chair should have several merits. Firstly, it should support you well. Its seat, backrest and armrests should fit your body, whatever position you sit in. The backrest of the chair should be sufficiently long, and once adjusted to your body, it should remain firm.

The seat should slope backwards to help you sit back in the chair, using the backrest for support. Once you have adjusted the backrest, you should be able to adjust your seat too. Seat depth, from the front of your chair to the back, must be adequate. The seat height must also be such that your feet rest comfortably on the floor. The seat front should be shaped so that the back portion of your knees do not feel any pressure. The seat should not tilt back when you have adjusted your backrest.

The armrests must be parallel to the seat and the floor and should easily be able to bear a part of your body weight.

Never pass a chair that has no support for the lower back, a short backrest or a nearly vertical backrest, a high front edge of the seat, a seat bottom that's soft in the centre creating a bucket effect.

A good worktable

The table should be of suitable height so that you do not strain the back while working. If it is too low, you might stoop during work. A desktop that has a slant or tilting top is ideal for reading and writing. It should also allow leg space under it to prevent undue arching forward of the back and the neck.

Beds, mattresses and pillows

Sleep is a superb health tonic. Good sleep recharges your battery and you wake up fresh as a daisy. But if you want a good night's sleep, invest in a good sleeping apparatus.

Make sure that the bed is supportive and comfortable. It should be firm enough to support your back, and at the same time soft enough to mould to the contours of your body and support its hollows and curves. A bed with a wooden board as its top, covered with a good 2-3-inch-thick mattress, which is soft but non-yielding and does not have any holes or indentations, makes an ideal choice.

A high-quality pillow is also vital for good sleep. It should be soft enough to mould around your neck and should be just the right height to keep the neck in neutral position. It should not be so high that the head is bent forward, nor should it be so big that your shoulders rest on it.

Instil the good habits early

The sooner a person picks up the good habits, the better it is for him or her. Thus, if you have young people at home, train them about the basics now. As a parent, teacher or elder, it is your responsibility to instil the basics of good posture so that the person does not suffer on this count.

Some tall children, particularly teenagers, develop a stoop out of shyness. Pull them out of this frame of mind, and ask them to stand up tall and confident. The merit of sitting up straight while working on a table or reading has already been extolled. To this, add the virtue of building good muscles by doing regular exercise. These measures should become an essential part of a child's life.

The stark truth is that most back problems result out of sloppy habits picked during early childhood years. In fact, some children also suffer painless micro-tears in the capsule of the intervertebral discs. You can prevent such mishaps by inculcating the value of preventive wisdom in the children.

As Feodor Dostoyevsky, a Russian writer, whose works carry profound psychological insight into the human behaviour, once wrote: "It seems, in fact, as though the second half of a man's life is made up of nothing but the habits he has accumulated during the first half." The key, therefore, is to catch the young ones early while they are still at an impressionable age, if you wish the backache clinics to close!

PART FOUR

Remedies and Cure

The sooner you pick the red flag that your troubled back unfurls, the better it is. The remedy lies in swift action, and not in acting when things get worse. Still, most people do themselves a disservice by neglecting the first signs of back trouble.

The treatment of an acute back problem is simple. Rest, analgesics, and cold-and-hot treatments often provide quick relief. However, as soon as you feel better, it's time to think ahead. Begin with gently mobilizing your stiff back and embark on a regular exercise plan. In the long run, a strong back is your best insurance

against back problems.

Managing chronic backache needs more careful thinking and you must be prepared to go the extra mile. While you make the most of treatments that can ease your pain, you must also set long-term goals and take steps to recognize and eliminate the culprits that first drove you down this misery lane.

Whether it be medication, physiotherapy, home-care measures, alternative medicine or surgery, the ultimate goal is to set yourself free so that you can savour the joys of life.

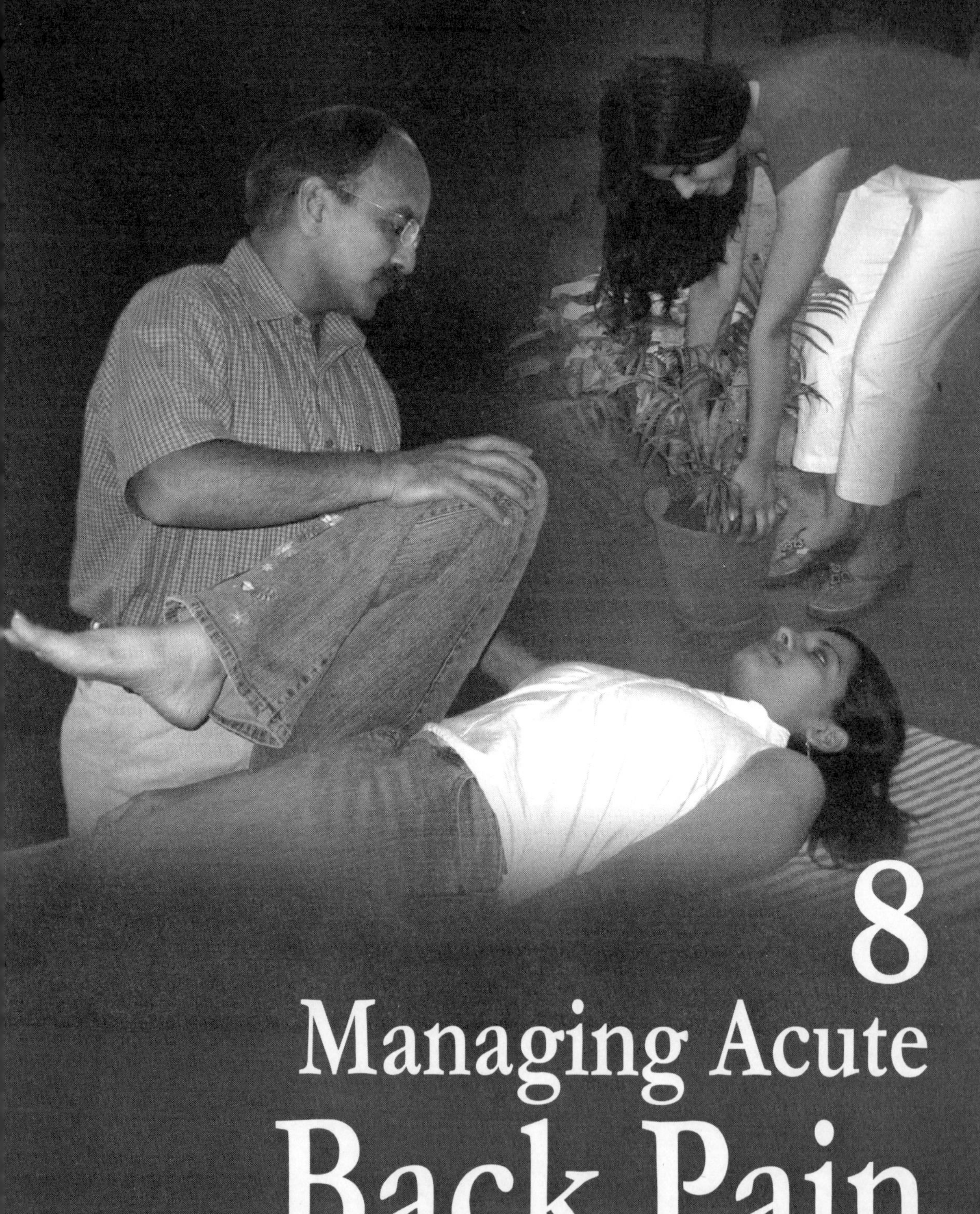

8
Managing Acute Back Pain

Acute back pain is often caused by a physical injury due to lifting heavy objects or to activities, such as digging in the garden. The pain is commonly caused by a strained muscle, tendon or ligament. The injury may be aggravated by subsequent activity.

Ordinarily, you should be able to treat the pain by taking simple home-care measures. In most cases, symptoms subside within two to ten days.

The fundamentals of treatment are best remembered by the acronym RAISE, where R stands for rest; A for analgesic (pain-relieving) pills and ointments; I for ice treatment; S for strapping the injured portion of the back; and E for exercises that hasten return to normalcy. After the first 48 hours, ice compresses can be substituted by heat treatment, using a heating pad or a wrapped hot water bottle.

While the back is on fire, you may take every step that reduces the pain. But vigorous massage and too much movement are best avoided, since they can worsen the pain.

Rest

The significance of rest in the treatment of an acute back has been known since long. The Egyptian physician-architect Imhotep, who is best known for creating the step-pyramid at Sakkara, was perhaps one of the first physicians to recognize that rest was the first recipe for treating backache. The logic is simple: rest allows the back injury to heal. If you neglect the injury, and stay up and work, you may easily aggravate the damage. Thus, sit, walk, climb or turn in bed at your peril, while a couple of days of comfortable rest in bed can ensure a quick recovery.

But do not stay in bed for more than two days. Start moving around as soon as possible and gradually return to normal activities.

Analgesic pills

Anti-inflammatory analgesics help relieve the pain and swelling. Until your back improves, they come in very useful. They work by blocking or reducing the sensation of pain and easing the inflammation. Several medications are available, and these include Aceclofenac, Diclofenac, Etodolac, Ibuprofen, Ketoprofen, Nimesulide, Naproxen, Piroxicam and Paracetamol. They may be taken singly or in combination with muscle relaxants, and must be taken in the prescribed dose. Most medications require to be taken two or three times a day.

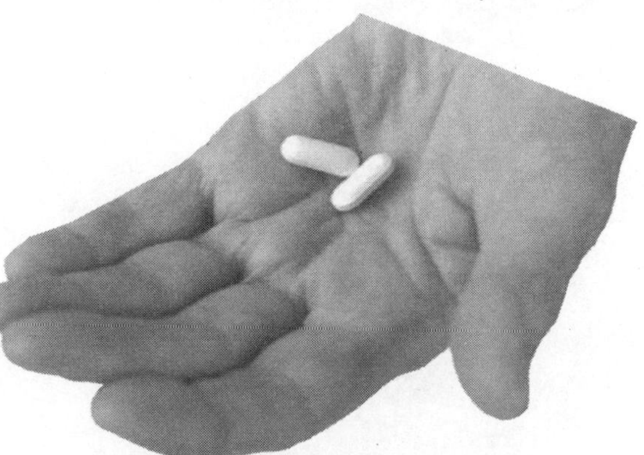

However, most analgesic pills have a drawback – they may cause mild to moderate adverse effects relating to the stomach. While many people suffer heartburn, abdominal bloating and gassy distension, some may also complain of nausea and vomiting. These unfavourable effects can be checked by pills that reduce the secretion of hydrochloric acid in the stomach.

Ice compresses

Cold treatments using ice or cold packs can help reduce the pain and swelling. To fashion an ice pack, roll a large cloth, old pillow cover or socks into a bag and fill it with ice chips. Now apply the pack to the painful part of the neck or back. If the pain and swelling relates to an acute muscle tear, this simple remedy will work well.

Heat treatment

Once the injury is older than 48 hours, it is best to switch to hot packs. Use a hot water bottle, heating pad, or infrared lamp. The application of heat treatment to the affected area stimulates blood flow, relaxes tense muscles and relieves pain. The treatment may be repeated three or four times a day.

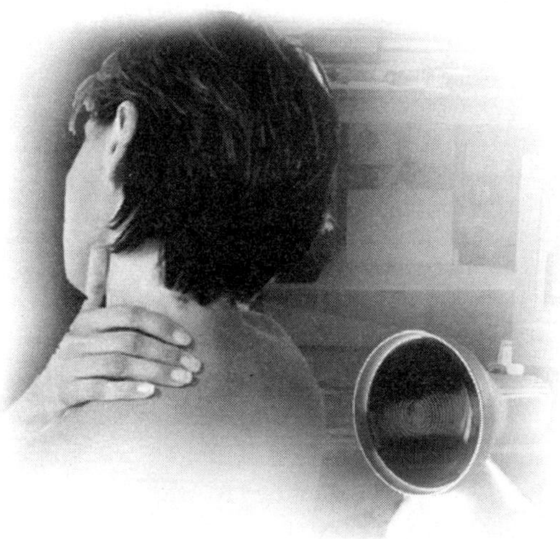

Gels and ointments

A number of analgesic and numbing agents are packaged as gels and ointments. There is not much to choose between them. You may use any of the preparations every few hours for its soothing effect. The best time to apply these formulations is soon after taking the heat treatment.

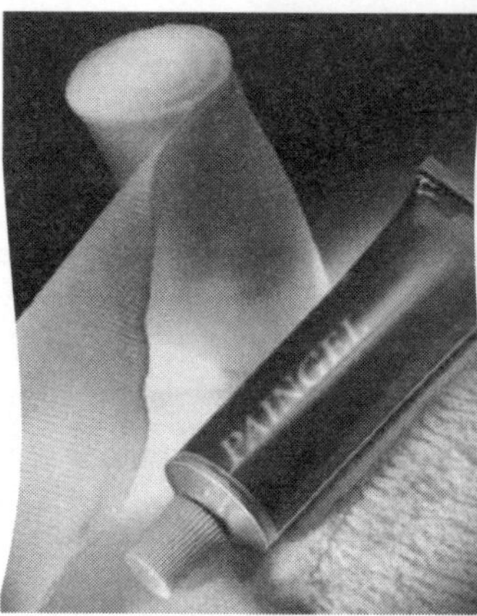

Belladonna tape

If the back harbours a tender area and is in acute spasm, consider the use of an adhesive tape impregnated with Belladonna and Capsicum. Keep the tape on for four or five days. It acts in three ways: one, it helps reduce the inflammatory swelling in the affected muscle planes; two, it works as a counter-irritant and numbs the pain; and three, it acts as a strapping.

Occasionally, however, the skin may react to the tape, leading to severe burning and rash. Thus, if you see any redness along the edges of the tape, it is best to remove it.

Strap your back

If a part of the lower back is painful, wobbly and tends to move too much when you bend over, or has lost its alignment, you may strap the back by wearing a lumbar support. It essentially consists of a firm body belt stretching from the rib cage to the pelvis with strengtheners behind, which may be flat steel strips moulded to the shape of the back. Wearing it would limit your back movements and help relieve back pain.

A neck collar can act in a like manner for a painful neck.

Exercises

Usually, the aim of exercise therapy is to strengthen the weak muscles and increase flexibility. It is best to gently mobilize the back. Simple exercises of the back and neck can begin in bed on the first day of the pain itself. Keep an eye on the movements to see if there is improvement. If you find the movements aggravate the pain or the pain is severe, you may wait for a day or two. Most back-care books do not recommend any exercise when you have an acute back pain, and several doctors also toe this line. But that's wrong. You are most likely to heed advice when you need it most, and you must consider making the exercise drill a part of your daily routine.

However, take care not go overboard. Go slow and carry out only the exercises that your doctor or therapist wants you to do. Do not rush into activities that may worsen the injury to the back. A gradual step-up approach works best. Over a period of days, there would be a steady improvement in the range of movement.

Before you begin the exercise programme, remember a few general guidelines:

- Always carry out only one movement at a time.
- Perform each exercise a maximum of five times and stop short if you feel any pain. However, you may do the circular movements of the shoulder 15 times.
- Relax for a count of five between each movement.
- During each active movement, inhale slowly to a count of five; and while returning to the position of rest, exhale slowly taking the same period of time.

The following exercises are known to

The back routine

Lie down straight on your back. Bend the right knee backwards towards the tummy, holding it with your hands. Hold. Return to the resting position. Now repeat the same step with the left knee. Repeat the drill five times.

Lie down straight on your back with both knees bent and both feet planted on the bed. Gently raise the hips, taking care that the back does not pain.

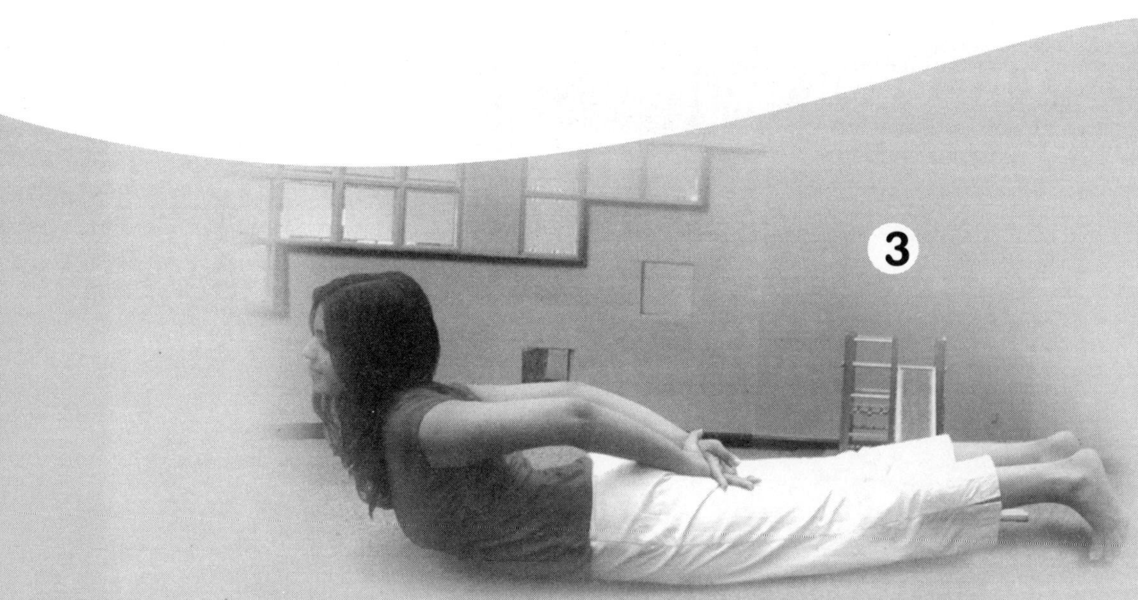

If you can turn over without feeling any pain, come to lie on your stomach with the face down. Rest your hands over the back. Now, raise the head and the chest a few inches.

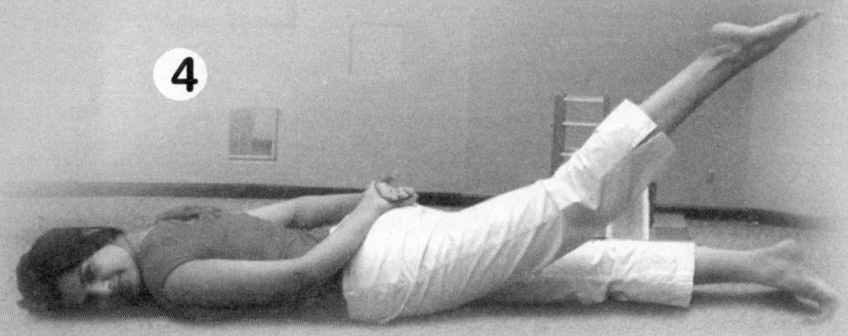

Continue to occupy the face-down position. Rest your hands over the back. Now, lift the right leg straight up at the hip without bending the knee. Hold. Return to the resting position. Now repeat the same movement with the left leg. Repeat the drill.

The neck drill

Motion exercises of the neck

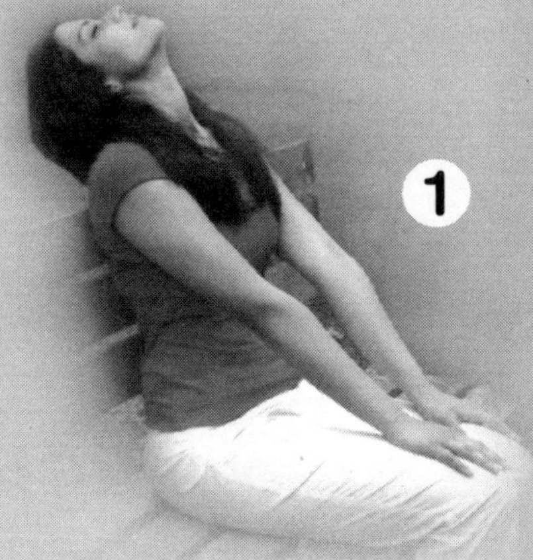

Sit up straight using a back support. Tilt the neck backward. Return to the neutral position.

Sit up straight. Turn the neck to the left, so that the chin approaches the shoulder. Return to the neutral position. Repeat the same movement of the neck to the right.

3

Tilt the neck to the left and down so that the ear approaches the shoulder. Return to the neutral position. Repeat the same movement of the neck to the right.

Circular movements of the shoulder

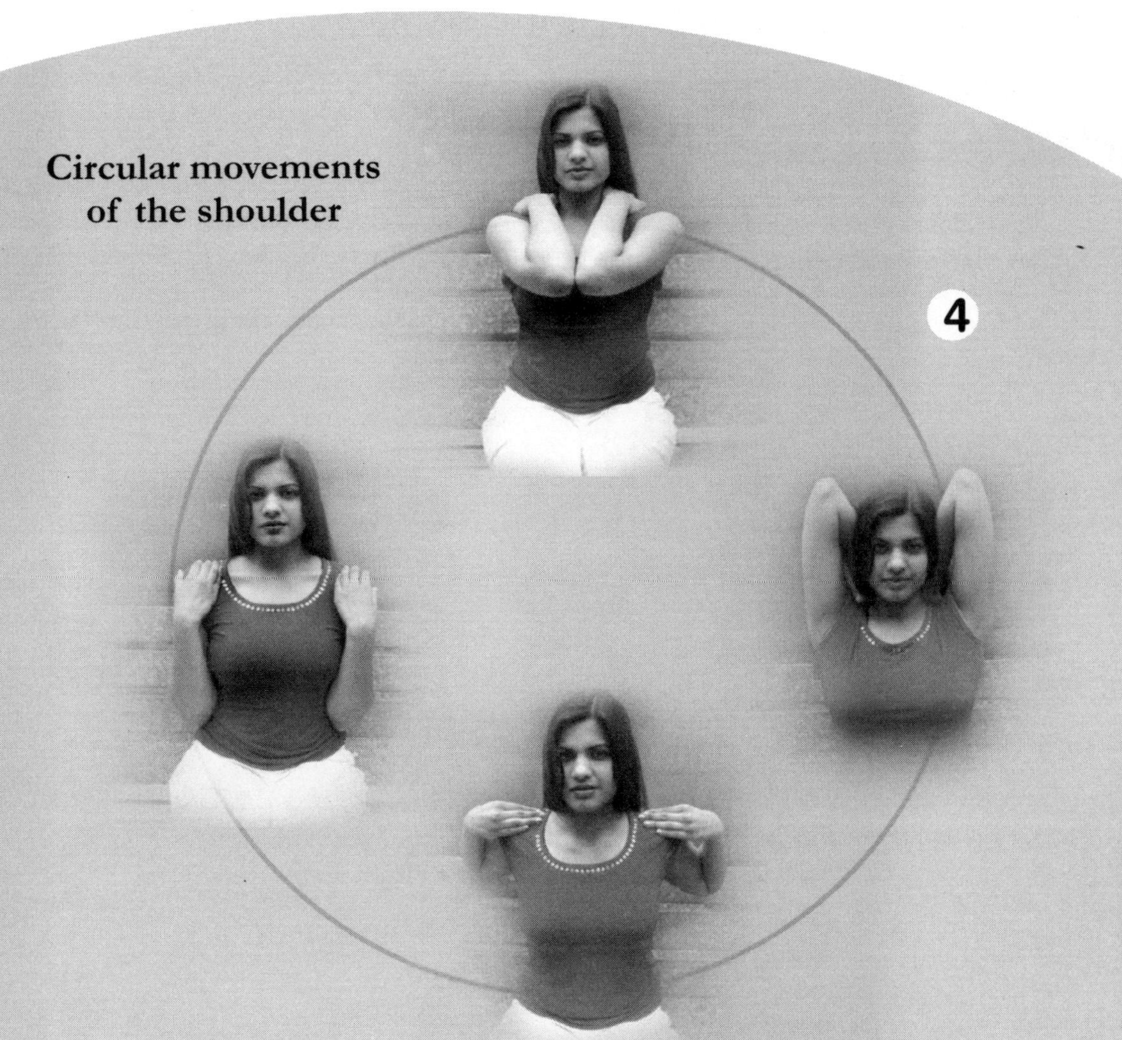

Bend both the elbows so that the fingers reach up to touch the shoulders. Now churn the shoulders in a slow motion to make a big arc, first forward and then backward 15 times. Gradually work towards augmenting the size of the arc.

The neck drill

Isometric exercises of the neck

Sit up straight. Using the left palm, apply pressure on the left cheek. Resist the turning movement of the neck by firming up the neck muscles and applying an equal neutralizing force. Hold. Return to the neutral position. Repeat the movement using the right palm against the right cheek.

Sit up straight. Using the left palm, apply pressure on the left temple. Resist the tilting movement of the neck by firming up the neck muscles and applying an equal neutralizing force. Hold. Return to the neutral position. Repeat the movement using the right palm against the right temple

7

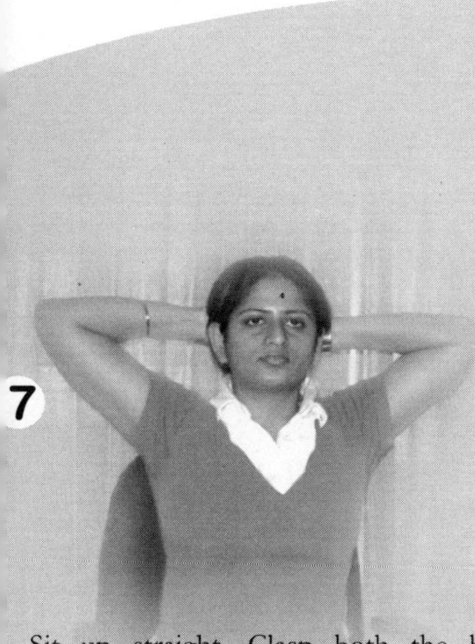

Sit up straight. Clasp both the hands together behind the head. Press the back of the head with your palms. Resist the forward movement of the neck by firming up the neck muscles and applying an equal neutralizing force.

Once you feel better, you are on the road to recovery. The exercises given above will help strengthen your back, neck and shoulders. If you do not feel any pain during the drill, it would be easier to return to normal daily activity.

Contrary to what you may think, normal activities like sitting, standing, bending, walking, lifting and climbing are much more strenuous than the prescribed exercise drill.

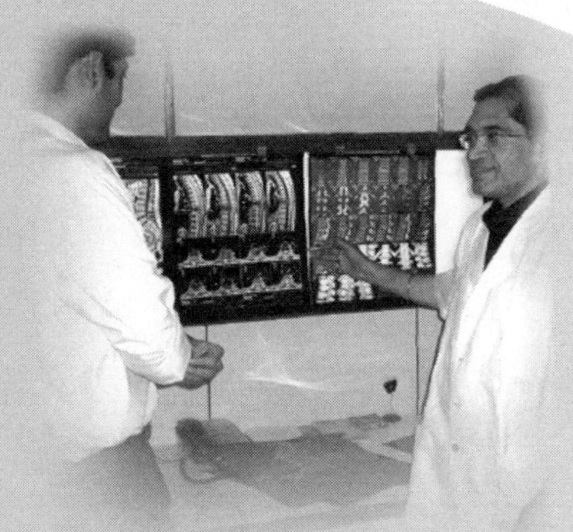

Consulting the doctor

In case the pain worsens or is too severe to allow you to move around after a few days, you should check with your doctor. You may have suffered more damage than you expected.

If you face symptoms that indicate possible nerve damage from a prolapsed disc, do not delay consulting your doctor. The following symptoms point to nerve damage:

- If you develop a problem with your bladder or bowel and seem to be losing control over them or suffer any numbness or loss of feeling in the groin or rectal area.
- If your leg or foot feels weak and you face difficulty in walking.
- If you have pain in the back that radiates down the leg with numbness or loss of feeling in the leg.
- If you have pain running down the leg and you experience repeated or prolonged 'pins and needles' in your leg.

9
Down the Recovery Lane

Once you have suffered an acute backache, think of it as a warning that your back needs regular maintenance. If you pay attention to posture, learn to lift correctly, and do regular exercises to strengthen the muscles of your back and make the spine more flexible, you may soon enough be fit to ride a horse. But if you are too busy or lazy to care for your back, you could soon be down in dumps, facing recurring attacks of back pain. The misery could easily multiply with the pain becoming chronic and ensnaring your life.

Yet, most people do not take notice when the back begins to fail. They simply keep delaying the protective maintenance of their backs, until they run into serious trouble. Sanjay's is a classical real life story. Let's look at it to understand how many of us slip up and let things run from bad to worse.

The real life story

Sanjay belonged to an average middle-class family. He was exceptionally hardworking and diligent. Through his sheer indus-triousness, he topped his batch at the business school. While still in his internship, during a campus interview he was picked by a finance company. Sanjay was intelligent, ambitious and a workaholic.

He quickly began to climb the corporate ladder. In no time, he was heading the division and in just a few years he became the general manager.

Sanjay's career graph was on a steep ascendancy. His board was happy with his 24 × 7 commitment, ability to think on his feet, and dynamism. He was being tipped to be the company's next vice-president. Not that he did not have any competition, Raj, a batchmate with a background similar to his, and a man no less brilliant was just a step behind in the race.

All seemed well until that evening. Sanjay was pottering in the garden – one of the few luxuries he still allowed himself occasionally. He decided to lift and move a flowerpot away from the passage. Before he could stand up, an excruciating back pain seized him. He barely managed to crawl back into his bed. Soon his old faithful Munna was by his side. He gave him a painkiller and applied a cold pack. But Sanjay knew he couldn't be up the next morning when a team of foreign financial investors was to visit their company. Raj would steal the march on him, he thought, but he could do little about it.

With the doctor's treatment, Sanjay soon felt better. He quickly returned to work, a tad earlier than his doctor preferred. Still, he quickly went back to his old ways, working late into the nights. If his back nagged him, he did not show. His management was appreciative of his work and six months later, he was given the responsibility he had long dreamt of. He was the new vice-president of the company. His batch-mate Raj quit and moved on.

Sanjay won the contest, but paid a terrible

price. His back was in bad shape, he had put on too much weight, his blood pressure had risen and the cholesterol level was high. Still, did he care? His family doctor warned him several times, but Sanjay did not keep the promises. Where was the time to do workouts and improve the fitness, when he began his day at 7a.m. and slept just before midnight.

Six months later, the pain became an essential part of Sanjay's life. If it got worse, he simply swallowed painkillers. He stopped bending or lifting objects and slept in a special bed. His physiotherapist told him he had chronic back pain, and he must learn to live with it. He also prescribed him a lumbar support. On his doctor's advice, Sanjay took an MRI test, which visualized the backbone, including the ligaments, discs, muscles and nerves. The test showed Sanjay had several discs bulging out of their place. The doctor warned him that unless he paid attention to his lifestyle, he might soon be a candidate for spinal surgery. The surgery shall only be a one-time remedy, and would not check further recurrences, the doctor told him.

Five years zipped by, and Sanjay became the president of his company. During this period, his back suffered further damage. He had several attacks of severe back pain, and twice he was hospitalised. The first time he barely managed to escape surgery. The MRI showed deterioration in two of the discs, which had ruptured and were pressing upon the spinal nerve roots. His physio worked hard to save him from going under the surgeon's knife. But the relief did not last long. Sanjay did little to mend his ways, and was laid up with severe pain. When despite resting in bed for two weeks things did not improve, and two of the toes on the right foot became numb, surgery became inevitable. Following the surgery, the pain became less, numbness also improved, but he still felt weak in the foot. He had to continue visiting the physio every fortnight. The pain was also not letting up, and would become more acute every now and again.

Sanjay was at the summit of his career. He had also been elected the chairman of Chambers of Commerce. He was scheduled to leave for Adelaide as the leader of a major business delegation. When he was leaving home, his son wished him well and said, "Dad, take care of your naughty back." Sanjay smiled and said, "Don't worry, sonny, I'll be okay." Little did he know he had spoken too soon.

At the airport, while checking in his luggage, without realizing what he was doing, he lifted the bag. Before he could place it on the counter, he collapsed in pain. How could he have been so naïve? His group rallied around, and the airport doctor was called. He was wheeled into the medical room and given a sedative shot. A short while later, Sanjay opened his eyes, to hear the airlines announcing his flight. His team members came up to console him and left. By then, his wife had also rushed to the airport and was at his side. He was taken to a hospital in an ambulance.

Finally, Sanjay's back had got back at him for years of neglect. There was no way to undo the damage now. Treatment would help him improve, but he was not getting any younger.

Stop…think…and act

Does this story ring a bell? Have you been trapped with similar experiences? If so, it is clearly time to stop, think and act. You must aim at doing better than Sanjay. Here's how to it:

Work on your fitness. Life is not just work, work and more work. It has much more to it. If you are ambitious, there is no harm in working hard, but make allowance for the body, mind and back fitness. Don't kill the basic instinct of self-preservation. Whatever be the compulsions of time, spend at least 30 minutes each day on your fitness. A brisk outdoor walk, brief work out at a gym, or walking on a treadmill at home can help you charge up your batteries and strengthen and limber your body.

Stay active. Keep up your activity. Regular outdoor activities like gardening, a game of badminton, tennis, squash, or basketball can get you moving and keep you physically fit. A high activity level also helps you improve your metabolism.

Remain trim. As you grow older, you tend to slack physically. This slows down your metabolism. Unless you make efforts to be active and cut down calories, it's hard to stay trim.

If you are overweight, make an extra effort to shed weight. Extra weight burdens the back and is generally bad for your health.

Never ignore the warning signs. The sooner you pick the red flag that your troubled back unfurls, the better it is. At the first twinge of back pain, sit up and think what you have been doing wrong. Is it your lifestyle, is it the posture, is it the furnishings, or is it too much work and stress? Try and get to the root of the problem and act before the damage magnifies.

Talk to a physio and occupational therapist. He or she can guide you about the posture, how to lift correctly, and also educate you on beds and pillows, worktable and chairs, and exercises that can help strengthen the weak muscles of the back. Under their guidance, you can make the spine more flexible.

Pay attention to the doctor's advice. Overruling the doctor may have its charm, but unless you only invest in short-term gains, that's not the way to go about health and life. If your back is in pain, do not risk further damage by returning to work earlier than the doctor's advice. Take proper treatment, let the back heal, and then resume work.

Think of health as a priority. Do not neglect your back, thinking that there will always be time later to make amends. This way you will never get round to restoring health, and before long it may be too late. You may end up paying a price that's too dear. By then, you could be the king of planet earth, but all the riches in the world would not buy you good health.

10
Winning Against Chronic Backache

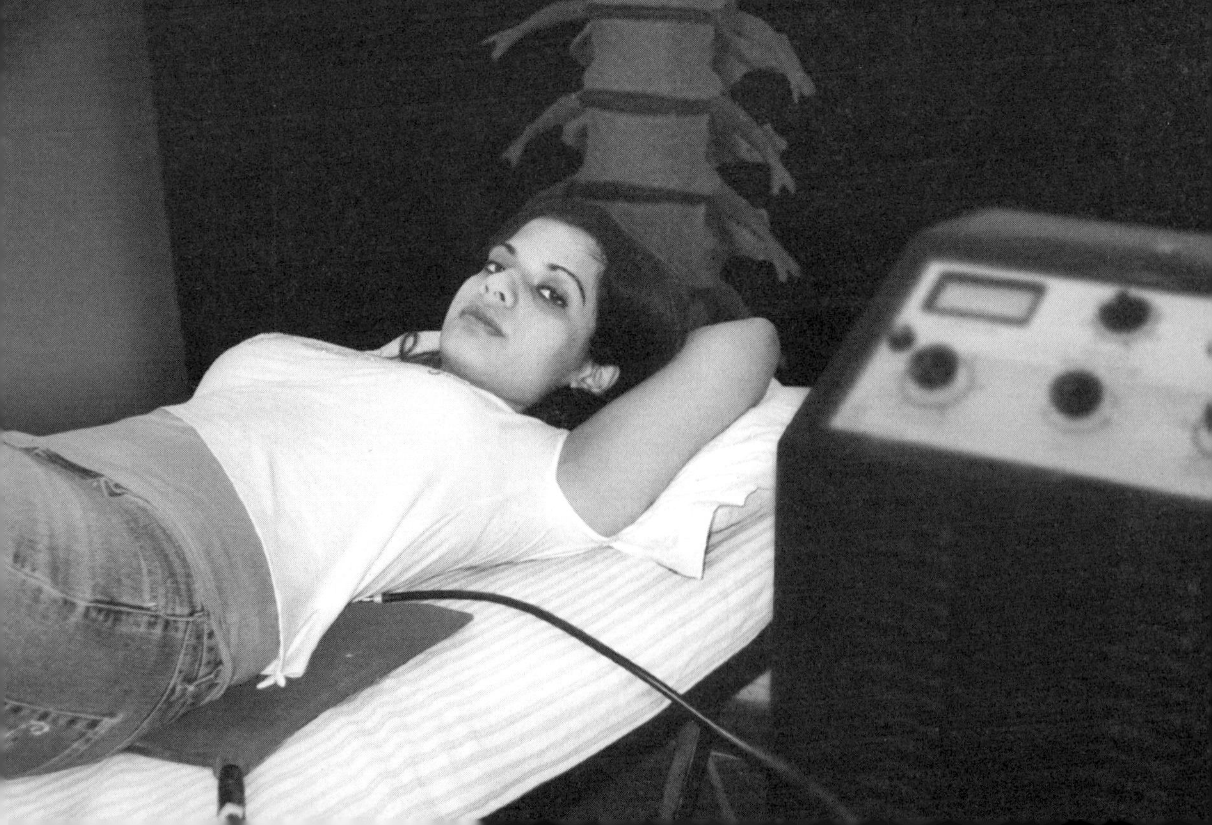

Winning against chronic backache is as much about knowing the fundamentals of back care as wearing the attitude of a champion. A '*sab chalta hai*' sentiment is just not the way out. Most people with chronic backache come to believe that they must now live with the handicap. But that's all in the mind. If you have the will, you could still be a champ.

The gravity of chronic backache can vary among people. While some fine-tune themselves to the changes and restrictions that must go hand in hand with their bad backs, many feel severely incapacitated and suffer a varying degree of compli-cations. While some may have numbness in toes, others may suffer a weak foot or be faced with a shooting pain in the limb. Some may find it difficult to sit, stand or walk for more than a few minutes, and yet others may pass sleepless nights and wake up to an extremely sore and aching back.

The trick lies in accepting the ordeal and working towards restoring your back to its pristine best. There would be times when you may feel like giving up, but that's not done. You must think like a champion and go all out to win.

The deal is simple, and here's how you can go about it.

Make peace with your body

Never overexert. If your body can take this much and no more, don't try to exceed its limit. Sit, stand, drive or walk only until it feels comfortable. If an activity causes pain, it is a clear signal of the body's distress. The idea is to make peace with your body, not dismiss the Mayday signal it is sending. Some people believe that by tolerating the pain and being brave, they can fool the body. But that's foolish. The way to be brave is to heed the red flag and in consultation with your treating doctor and physio, plan ahead and gradually restore the strength and flexibility of your back. By and by, you could soon be surpassing your old self and setting yourself on a winning course.

Unburden your back

If your back is in bad shape and you feel pain every time you move, the situation calls for more radical measures. Try and unburden your back. Rest in bed. That is the best single posture that loads the back the least. Once you feel better, you can turn in bed or stand for a few minutes. Contrary to what you may expect, sitting up burdens the back more than if you were to stand. Bending, climbing and lifting can certainly wait till you are back to normal.

Pay no heed to amateurish advice

When you are laid up with back pain, several relatives and friends may visit you. While some may bolster your confidence and offer you solace, others may talk negatively and narrate you the worst possible experiences. They may also offer several treatments and advice. Do not be carried away by what they say; they all may mean well, but you need to listen to your doctor and nobody else.

If you think a particular recipe may be worthy of consideration, talk to your doctor about its possible effectiveness.

Determination is the key

Most chronic back pain patients despair of their condition. They fear that the problem would live with them for life and that they would be faced with severe restrictions in life. Some doctors also contribute to such a mindset by handing a big list of dos and don'ts, and not telling how long you have to follow them.

You must not leave room for despondency. If you make a sincere effort to get better, change your way of life, work to strengthen the muscles and improve the flexibility of your spine, it is just a question of time before you would be well and truly on the road to recovery.

Here's one real life story that may perk you up and you may think it worthy of emulating.

The real life story

This is about a New York fireman, who lost his job to a bad back. He had worked very hard in his younger years and had earned rightful respect of his colleagues and the chief, before his back began to trouble him. The problem became so acute that he could scarcely work for a few weeks, before he would report sick and be laid up for several days. The man lost his efficiency, his speediness to act, and could not meet the demands of his high-pressure job. Reluctantly, the chief called him one day to his office, recalled the long years of selfless service he had put in for the community, and told him he would be much better off by moving to a less-demanding job.

The man had never considered this option. Proud and devoted to his profession, he felt deeply hurt at losing the job. But he did not take a moment to give in his papers for seeking premature retirement. While he did so, a new resolve lit up in him. He must defeat the problem that had taken his job away. His steely determination helped him gradually overcome the bad back. His old self once more, he decided to prove his mettle. He proceeded to participate in the big annual marathon race of the city, which involved racing up the tallest building in New York, the Empire State Building. He did, and was the *winner.*

Choose you doctor with care

Depending on where you live, you may decide to rely upon a back-care specialist, an orthopaedic surgeon, a physiatrist or the family physician for being your primary doctor. But choose you doctor with care. He or she must be knowledgeable, experienced, positive-minded and not too rushed.

Once you begin the treatment, avoid changing the doctor unless there are compelling reasons. Each doctor works differently. If you change doctors mid way, it is like starting again. You lose on time, money and effort, and delay your recovery.

Specialized centres work best

The treatment of chronic back pain is best carried out by a multi-speciality team. If you can afford to go to a treatment centre that offers the services of an orthopaedic surgeon, a physiatrist, physiotherapist, neurologist, clinical psychologist and pain specialist all under the same roof, it may be best. A team such as that can address all your problems, without you having to run from one treatment facility to another.

Fact file

Dr Vernon Nickel, an orthopaedic surgeon working at the Rancho Los Amigos Medical Centre, Southern California, was the first to introduce the concept of rehabilitative care in the 1950s. His broad vision of rehabilitation covered all physical disabilities, and stepped beyond the traditional confines of orthopaedics. Nickel's treatment was accomplished through a team approach and was organized around the specific needs of the patient. He integrated the services of surgeons, internists, nurses, physical therapists, occupational therapists, speech therapists and social workers to look at all aspects of a patient's life to determine which treatment would work best to return the patient to active life. His methods helped many polio patients under institutional care return to mainstream life and become independent.

Significance of the tests

Your doctor may ask for a number of laboratory and radiological tests. These may include X-rays, blood test, urine test, CT scan and the MRI. If a test comes up with a finding, do not read too much into it unless you have discussed the results with your treating doctor. Several tests may be falsely positive, and their significance must be viewed in the light of clinical symptoms and signs. Even modern-day expensive tests, like the MRI, suffers from this drawback.

Medications

Analgesics

If you are in pain, consider taking the non-steroidal anti-inflammatory pills that your doctor ordered. They can relieve you of pain and help you relax. A number of medications can provide you relief, and you may indicate to your doctor if a particular medicine works better for you than other pills. Some doctors might not like this, and think that you are interfering with their job. But if you know what's good for you, don't hesitate in revealing your preference.

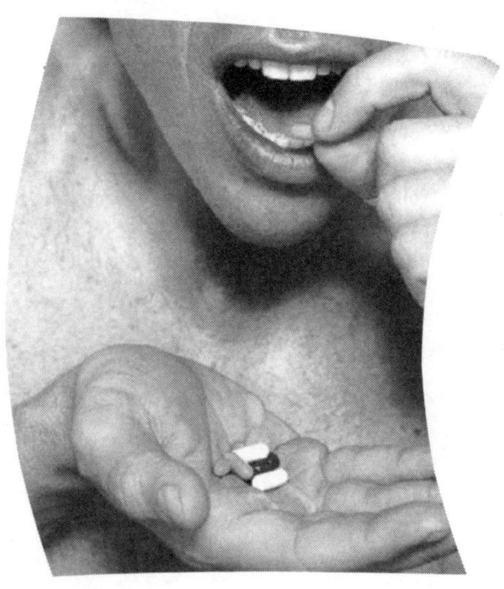

The biggest drawback with these medications is the distressing adverse effect related to the stomach. You may suffer heartburn, abdominal bloating and gaseous distension. You could mitigate these effects by taking anti-ulcer drugs that reduce the secretion of acid in the stomach.

Once you feel better, you can talk to your doctor and gradually reduce the dose, before finally stopping the medication. If you find it difficult to pop pills every six or eight hours, ask your doctor about the option of extended or sustained release preparations that can be taken once or twice daily.

You should avoid stopping the anti-inflammatory pills mid way. Do not be misled by the belief that they are simply painkillers and must not be taken for more than a few days. If you feel better, discuss with your doctor before you stop them. He or she may like to gradually taper the dose, and not stop it all of a sudden. You run the risk of rebound-pain, if you let go of the pills suddenly.

Usually the best time to stop the medication is when you have recovered the flexibility and strength of the muscles and can engage in your normal day-to-day activities.

Muscle-relaxant pills and ointments

To relieve the tightness and spasm in the lower back muscles, your doctor may advise you to take muscle-relaxant pills. Some also advocate pain-relief gels and ointments. The latter can be rubbed gently on the back. They generate warmth in the area and give a soothing effect. Some people also find relief with the water-absorbing and counter-irritant effect of Belladonna plaster. Try it out.

Physical therapy

Before you begin with active physiotherapy and start doing exercises, your back muscles must be relieved of the pain and spasm. The physio

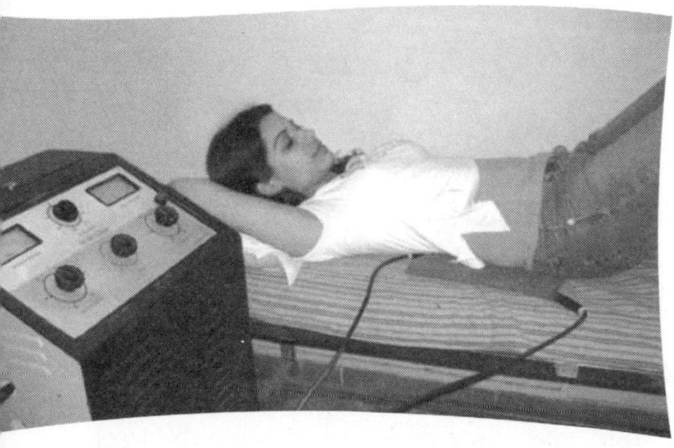

can help you in this mission by offering diathermy (heat pad) and ultrasonic therapy over the tender areas.

Short-wave diathermy

Short-wave diathermy works best to treat sore muscles and joints, which lie in the deeper plane of the body. The technique is simple and pain-free. The part to be treated is placed between two condenser plates, and the temperature of the subcutaneous tissues is raised.

Ultrasonic therapy

Ultrasonic therapy uses high-frequency sound waves. Their heating effect improves

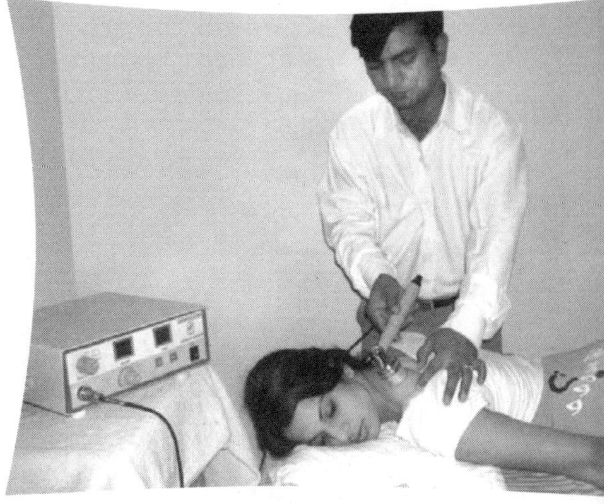

circulation and helps speed up the rate of ion diffusion across cell membranes. It is used to treat the muscles, tendons and ligaments that are too deep to be significantly affected by heat packs.

During the treatment, a hand-held microphone-like device is moved slowly across the area that needs the treatment. The procedure is completely painless.

Assisted exercises

Once your pain gets controlled, the physio may try to help you by starting passive assisted exercises. By doing gentle movements, he or she may be able to stretch the tight muscles out. Once the muscles become supple, she may help you do assisted movements. The movements aim at putting different muscle groups to use. In time, she may put you through a full range of movement.

Active exercises

Once you have come thus far, the onward road is easy. You must now try and do the exercises without the help of your therapist. Gradually, you would notice the improvement: activities that brought you pain would now be quite easy to carry out.

While doing any exercise, if you do not feel any pain, try and hold the position in which a particular muscle is in a contracted state for a count of five. This will help the muscles to gradually become strong. You may also work at enhancing your endurance. Repeat each exercise five times.

Once you feel strong, spend 15 minutes every day to exercise. You can also begin the exercises described in Chapter 8.

The role of exercise and physiotherapy is paramount. You must now work at stretching the taut hamstrings and strengthening the lax abdominal muscles, and improve their flexibility. You may begin by doing the exercises under the supervision of a physiotherapist, but once you feel sure, you can do them at home.

Stretching the hamstrings

The hamstrings that run all along the back of the thigh often become too tight. This puts a lot of stress on the lower back.

You can easily overcome this difficulty by carrying out a simple stretch of the muscles.

Lie down straight on your back. Now hold your right thigh with one hand and the calf with the other, and try and bring the knee close to the stomach. Once you have done this, try and gradually straighten the knee as far as is comfortable. Slowly, over a period of few weeks, you may be able to raise the leg at 90 degrees to the back. Do the exercise first on the right side and then the left, repeating each manoeuvre five times each.

Strengthening the abdominal muscles

The abdominal muscles are crucial for the health of the back, but if you are overweight, your abdominal muscles are likely to be weak. You may wear the stance of a lord, but the posture will stress the back. The inter-vertebral disc also may suffer damage. If you wish to guard against these problems, the simplest way is to strengthen the abdominal muscles.

Doing sit-ups will make your abdominal muscles strong. Lie down straight on your back. Keep your hands against the shoulders. Bend the knees. Now, try and raise the upper trunk and chest. At first it may be difficult, but gradually the muscles become strong and you can rise rather easily. When you rise, breathe out. Breathe in while you return to the floor. Repeat the exercise five times.

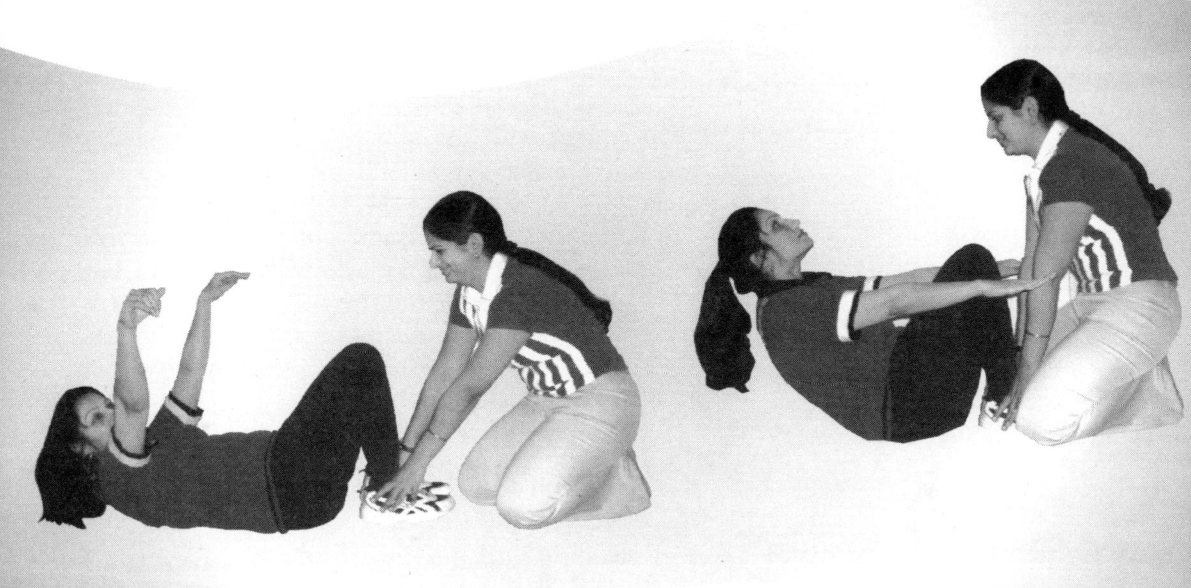

If you find it difficult, try a little variation. Stretch the hands out on the sides rather than keeping them against the shoulders. You may find this easier to do.

Traction

Hippocrates, the father of modern medicine, is credited with devising the earliest system of traction for the spine in the treatment of back pain. The method would raise goose pimples today. The ankles of the patient were tied to the lowest rung of a ladder, and the ladder was then raised upside down by two well-endowed attendants, so that the patient would lie suspended feet up. The ladder could also be raised by about a foot and was then jerked down. This gave a sudden jolt to the back and brought the joints into normal alignment.

Today, much more sophisticated traction systems exist. But the basic principle remains the same. The troubled portions of the back are gently stretched to relieve the spasm of the back muscles and stretch the arthritis-ridden joints so as to ease the pressure on the spinal nerves.

The method is simple. You lie straight

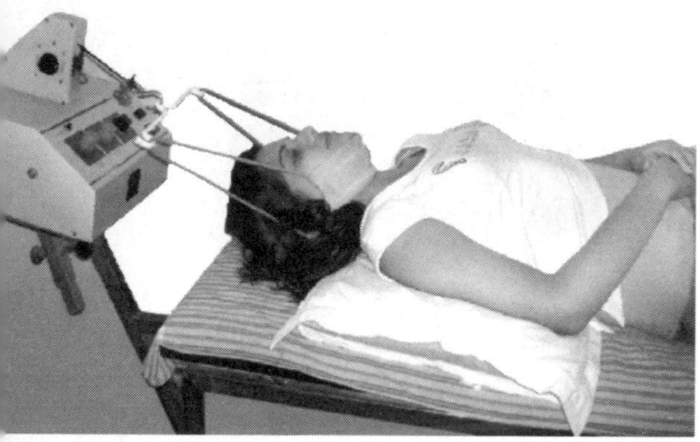

on a traction table. While one harness goes around the lower chest, the other goes around the pelvis, and the system pulls the two halves of the body gently apart. A timer ensures that the physio keeps your back under traction for just about the right period of time.

You can also apply traction at home. You may consider dangling straight down on your arms from the top of a door. At the other end of the scale there are various sorts of specialised devices that you can use to apply traction while you lie straight on the bed. Separate devices are available for giving traction to the neck. The safest course however is to undergo traction under the watchful supervision of a physiotherapist.

Belts, corsets and braces

A wide variety of supports are available for a weak back. Belts, corsets and braces, which come in all shapes and sizes and made out of the latest materials, can be worn as supports during sitting, travelling and climbing while you are still recovering from a bad back.

But you must not use them for too long. The supports do offer some relief, but also impede the strengthening of the back and abdominal muscles. It is best to use them for short periods to tide over a difficult period.

Steroid shots into the epidural space

If nothing else works or some residual pain continues to bother you, your doctor might consider giving you a steroid injection into the spinal epidural space. The procedure needs some expertise, and is best carried out in the

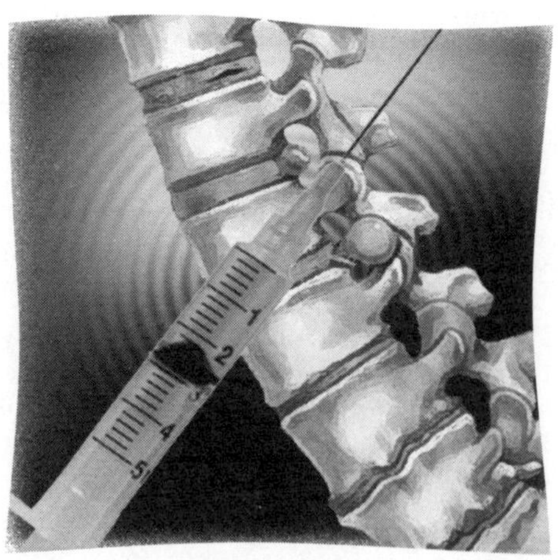

sterile setting of an operating room. The doctor pushes a long-acting corticosteroid along with a local numbing agent into the epidural space of the lumbar or sacral region of the spine. The shot helps provide relief by reducing the swelling in the back where one or more degenerative discs are pressing against the ligaments and spinal nerve roots. If given at the correct site, it works well as a potent adjuvant therapy, and can be repeated two to three times at intervals of 10-14 days.

Blocks for arthritic joints

The steroid shots do not offer significant relief in people who have pain arising from arthritis of the intervertebral joints. Such patients may best be served by pushing a numbing agent into the arthritic joint under specialized X-ray equipment, such as a C-arm image intensifier or a CT scanner. While the affected part is under direct radiological vision, the doctor pushes the drug into the diseased joint.

When to consider surgery

Less than one per cent of chronic backache patients require spinal surgery. Others do equally well with non-operative treatment. The patients who may benefit with early spinal surgery are those who suffer acute compression of nerve roots and reveal signs of severe progressive weakness and numbness in the fingers or toes. In such cases, surgery may check serious nerve damage and help restore normal sensation and function to the limb. Several types of surgeries are done, of which microscopic removal of the disc (micro discectomy) and endoscopic discectomy are the most popular.

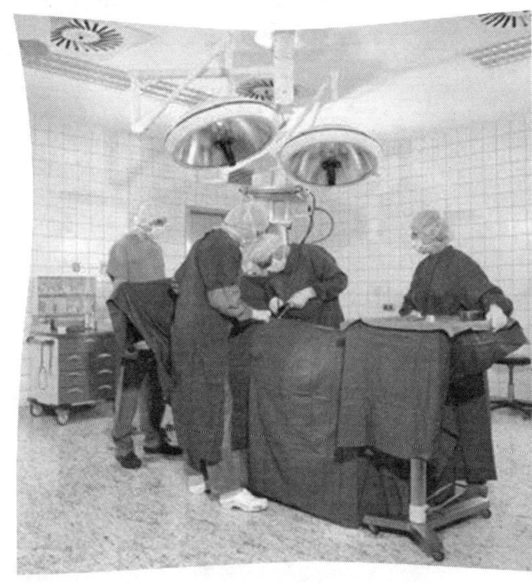

Watch out for the red flags

If faced with a back pain that's associated with symptoms that may point to another illness, such as cough, loss of appetite, weight loss, constipation, chronic diarrhoea, vomiting, bleeding, difficulty in passing urine, you may consider going for a thorough check-up to find out the root cause of your symptoms. Sometimes back pain may be a fall-out of a disease like tuberculosis, osteoporosis or spread of cancer to bones of the spine. If your doctor prescribes any tests, such as X-rays of the spine, blood test including complete blood counts, ESR, liver function tests, and serum electrophoresis, bone scan, and a MRI, view them in this light. The tests may not yield anything exciting, but that's always good news.

Staying in control

Once you are out of the woods, it is time to think ahead. Make a long-term plan so that you may never have back pain again. This may call for making several changes in life. There are simply no shortcuts. Unless you make a determined effort, you are likely to suffer again. The rules are as follows:

- Stick to a regular exercise schedule to tone up your body and improve its flexibility, strength and endurance. Find time for it, whatever else you may not do.
- Pay attention to your posture, particularly, when you bend to lift an object.
- Invest in an ergonomically sound office and home furniture. Recurrence of back pain is a high price to pay for a sloppy backrest, low chair or worktable, or poor bed and mattresses.
- Keep motoring on this road to good health. Never ever think of lowering the guard.
- If you wish to raise the bar, and perform physically demanding tasks, you must work to achieve the peak physical fitness. Carry out regular physical exercise, go for outdoor sports and think positive. A healthy lifestyle and positive attitude are fundamental to preventing future episodes of back pain.

Alternative therapies

A variety of indigenous systems of medicine, including acupuncture, ayurveda, yoga, Unani, homeopathy, naturopathy, osteopathy and chiropractic are practised widely all over the world. They have been used with a varying degree of success in refractory patients of chronic backache. It may be difficult to explain their functional worth and relate them to the definitions of modern-day science, but that they are effective and provide relief to the patient is the best validation of their usefulness. Many pain clinics offer acupuncture and acupressure services to the patients, and there is nothing wrong if the accupuncturist is careful about using a set of fresh sterile needles in each patient.

Yoga can also help in many ways. While some yogic exercises promote flexibility, endurance, and improvement in postures of the body, others like deep breathing exercises help release stress.

A holistic approach allows combining the goodness of each system of medicine for relieving the patients of their illness.

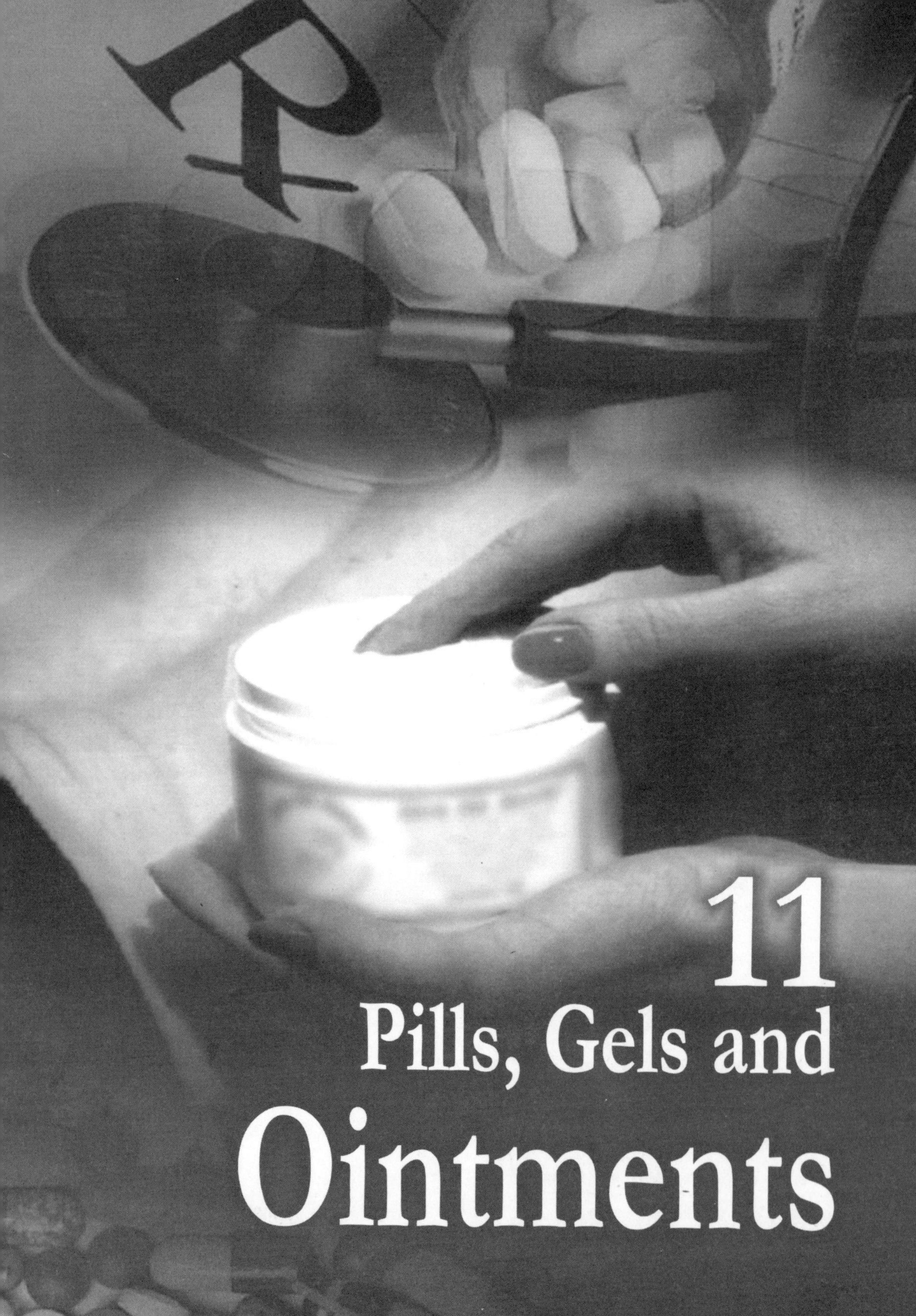

11
Pills, Gels and Ointments

The role of medicines in back treatment is to relieve pain, prevent further damage and promote normal function. You may be asked to use a variety of pills, gels, ointments, and rarely shots to make good a recovery. Many of these preparations are available over-the-counter with the chemist, but it is best to follow the doctor's advice.

While writing a prescription, your doctor carefully considers your condition, the peculiarities of your system, if you have any, such as any another illness, and weighs the risks and benefit ratio of each medicine that he writes. If a drug is very potent but has serious side effects, he is not likely to prefer it to a drug that's less potent but has no or few side effects. Clearly, the idea is to benefit you, not accentuate your suffering. Still, if you have a problem, speak to your doctor. He may decide to replace the drug, adjust its dose, or change its timing.

Some people are sceptical about the usefulness of medicines. That's not good. Medicines can help make your life pain-free and active again, as long as you take them with proper care and follow your doctor's instructions.

Non-steroidal anti-inflammatory drugs (NSAIDs)

NSAIDs are a group of medicines that are used to relieve pain and swelling (inflammation), particularly of muscles, ligaments, and joints. They form the mainstay of treatment in both acute and chronic forms of back pain.

When used in the treatment of an acute back pain that develops suddenly, such as due to ligament damage and muscle strains and tears, they usually reduce symptoms within a few hours.

They also help relieve pain and inflammation caused by long-term chronic back pain that develops following the wear and tear changes caused by osteoarthritis in the spine. When used to treat this condition, they rapidly relieve pain, but may take about two weeks to reduce inflammation.

Although NSAIDs are effective in alleviating symptoms, they do not cure the underlying condition.

Common medicines

Diclofenac, Etodolac, Fenoprofen, Flurbiprofen, Ibuprofen, Indomethacin, Ketoprofen, Mefenamic acid, Nabumetone, Naproxen, Piroxicam and Sulindac.

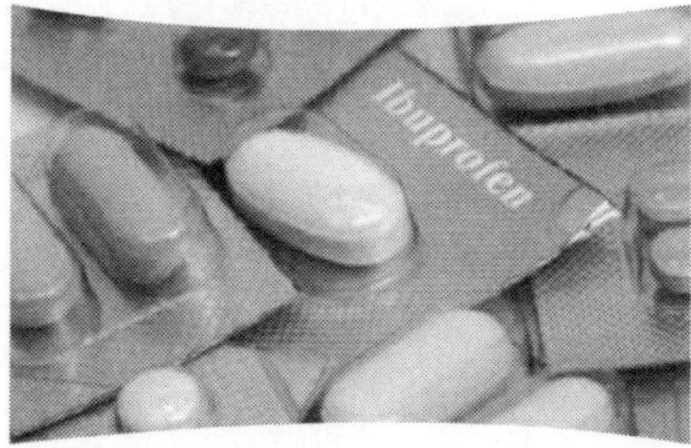

Mechanism of action

These medicines work by limiting the release of prostaglandins or chemicals occurring naturally in the body that cause pain and trigger the inflammatory response.

How are they used?

Commonly taken by mouth in the form of pills, they are best consumed after meals. Occasionally they may also be applied as a gel or given by an injection. Certain formulations are available in a slow-release form, which may be effective for up to 24 hours. This reduces the need to take pills frequently when long-term conditions are being treated.

Side effects

Most NSAIDs are safe, but they can cause a variety of side effects. They all irritate the stomach lining to a varying degree. If you are to use them for long, you would be best advised to also use an antiulcer drug such as Pantaprazole to protect your stomach lining. Some people also complain of abdominal discomfort due to irritation of the bowel.

They may also cause allergic reactions, including rashes and a condition known as angio-neurotic oedema, in which temporary, painless swellings develop in the skin and mucous membranes. Some people may develop photosensitivity, in which the skin becomes abnormally sensitive to sunlight. Some people also feel dizzy and light-headed. NSAIDs can also cause fluid retention, increase the blood pressure, and worsen a pre-existing heart failure.

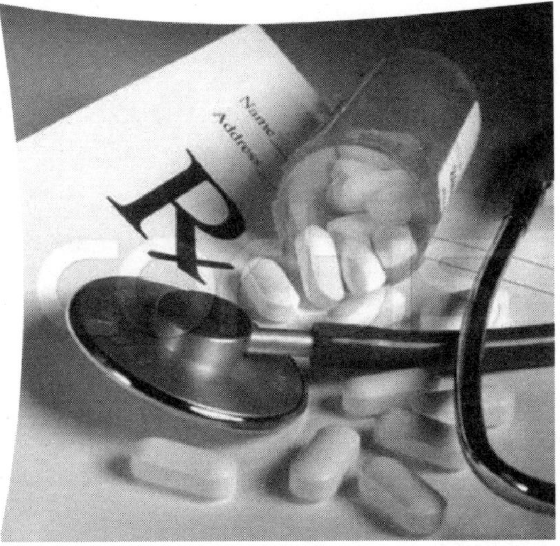

People who have asthma or kidney disorder are advised to avoid them since they can make the condition worse.

Opioid Painkillers

Opioid painkillers are mainly used to relieve severe pain. They play a significant role in the treatment of acute back pain after the initial injury, and are also used to treat severe episodes of chronic back pain.

Common medicines

Codeine, Fentanyl, Pentazocine and Morphine.

Mechanism of action

Opioids act on the brain, thus stopping the transmission of pain. These medicines work in a similar way to natural substances called endorphins, which are released in the brain in response to pain.

How are they used?

Opioids may be taken orally or, if the pain is very severe or accompanied by vomiting, may be given by injection.

Side effects

Prolonged use of opioids may lead to dependence. However, you are very unlikely to become dependent if you take them for a few days to relieve severe pain.

Side effects include constipation, nausea, vomiting, and drowsiness. Larger doses can depress breathing and may also cause confusion and dull the senses. An overdose can be fatal.

Nonopioid Painkillers (Analgesics)

Analgesics are a group of medicines that are used to relieve pain.

Common medicines

Paracetamol, Acetaminophen and Aspirin.

Paracetamol

Often used for relieving fever, Paracetamol or Acetaminophen is a useful pain-relief pill. You can get it at over-the-counter without a doctor's prescription. The dose varies according to the severity of pain. You might take one or two 500 mg Paracetamol tablets every six hours and it is quite safe.

However, if you are sensitive to Paracetamol, or suffer from asthma, peptic ulcer, alcohol-related liver disease, or use a blood thinner (anticoagulant), you need to be careful.

Aspirin

Aspirin is another commonly used painkiller with a mild anti-inflammatory effect. It can be used to treat mild to moderate back pain.

However, Aspirin can cause severe side effects. While indigestion and abdominal upsets are common, it can also cause ringing noises in the ears and affect hearing if used over a long period. In high doses, it can produce dangerous toxic effects.

Colchicine

Colchicine is an anti-gout compound, but can sometimes prove very useful in patients who are faced with severe backache that does not respond to the regular pain-relief pills and tablets.

Colchicine is however used sparingly because it carries a high probability of sev-ere side effects. Nausea, vomiting, diarrhoea and abdominal pain are the common refrains of people who take Colchicine.

Anticonvulsants

Anticonvulsants are generally used to prevent the recurrent seizures in epilepsy, but they are also used to treat sharp shooting pain caused by nerve damage. Some people who suffer from sciatica due to a prolapsed disc may benefit

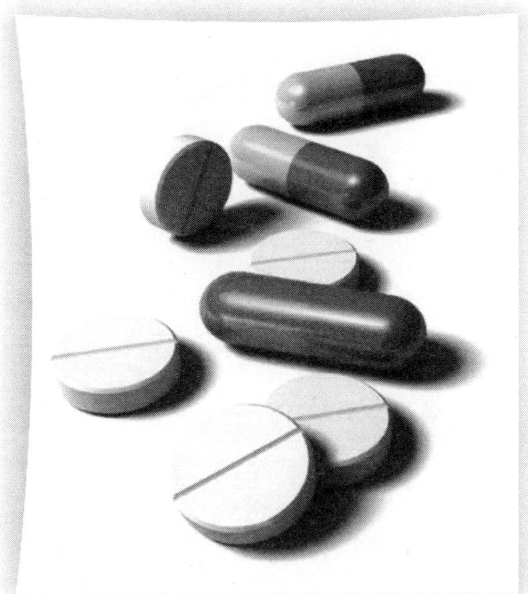

by using Carbamazepine, a commonly preferred anticonvulsant.

Common medicines

This group includes a variety of medicines but Carbamezapine is most commonly used when treating pain due to nerve damage.

How are they used?

Anticonvulsants are taken orally. Their dose is adjusted so that the medicine controls the pain without causing unwanted side effects.

Side effects

Anticonvulsants can affect memory and coordination. They may produce lethargy and weaken concentration. You should consult your doctor if you develop an infection, because some anticonvulsants reduce the effectiveness of the immune system. If you are planning to become pregnant, talk to your doctor before you decide.

Muscle relaxants

Muscle relaxants are used for alleviating muscle stiffness and spasms – a painful, involuntary contraction of one or more muscles, a feature commonly found in acute back strain or sprain. They are also useful in the treatment of fibrofasciitis.

Common medicines

Carisoprodol, Chlorzoxazone, Methacarbamol, Tizanidine and Diazepam.

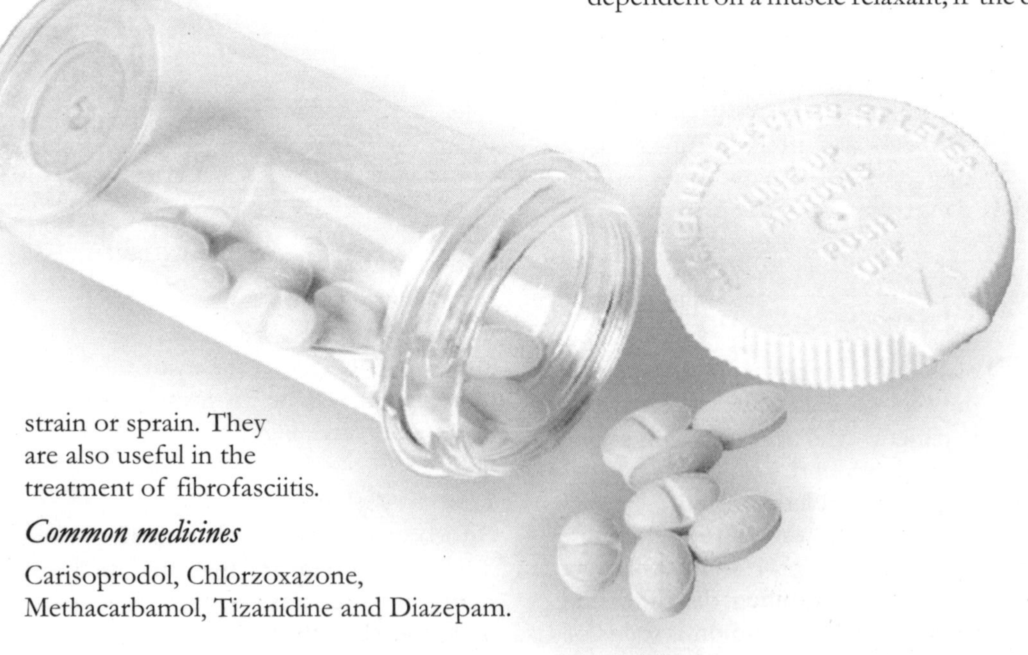

Mechanism of action

Muscle relaxant medicines mostly work by reducing transmission of nerve signals from the brain and spinal cord to the muscles, causing the muscles to relax.

How are they used?

Doses of muscle relaxants need careful adjustment as too little has no effect, while too much leads to muscle weakness. They are mostly required to be taken at eight-hourly intervals to be effective and are best used only for a few days after the initial injury in combination with NSAIDs.

Side effects

Drowsiness is a common side effect with muscle relaxants. Once you have taken them, you must not drive or go near heavy machines to prevent an accident. With long-term use, the body may become dependent on a muscle relaxant; if the drug is withdrawn suddenly, muscle spasmsmay become worse than they were before treatment began.

Antidepressants

Antidepressants are medicines that are generally used to treat the symptoms of depression. Though they do not have any useful role in acute back pain, they benefit those people who suffer from regional fibromyalgia and fibromyalgia syndrome. They are also indicated if you feel depressed and cannot sleep because of chronic back pain.

Common medicines

Amitryptiline, Doxepin, Fluoxetine, Imipramine and Sertraline are the most commonly prescribed antidepressants in the treatment of back pain.

Mechanism of action

Antidepressants work by helping to restore certain chemicals called neurotransmitters in the brain. These chemicals are thought to increase brain activity and improve one's mood.

How are they used?

Antidepressants are taken orally. You must take them at least for one to three weeks before they can have any positive effect on you.

Side effects

Side effects vary with the choice of medicine. While some may cause a dry mouth, blurring of vision, constipation, difficulty in passing urine and rapid heartbeat, others lead to nausea, diarrhoea, nausea, vomiting, reduced sex drive and headache.

Locally-acting corticosteroids

Corticosteroids are chemicals similar to the natural Corticosteroid hormones produced by the body. Their main use is to relieve the inflammation in the soft tissues and joints. In back pain patients, they are sometimes used as locally-acting injections in the epidural space and intervertebral joints. They are effective in blocking acute back pain or an acute flare up of chronic back pain when other medications are not able to provide any relief.

Common medicines

Betamethasone, Dexamethasone, Hydrocortisone, Methylprednisolone and Triamcinolone.

Mechanism of action

Corticosteroids block the immune response that triggers production of natural substances that cause inflammation and pain in the body.

How are they used?

They are injected into the epidural spaces around the membranes surrounding the spinal nerves in the spinal canal to provide relief in patients who suffer from sciatic nerve pain

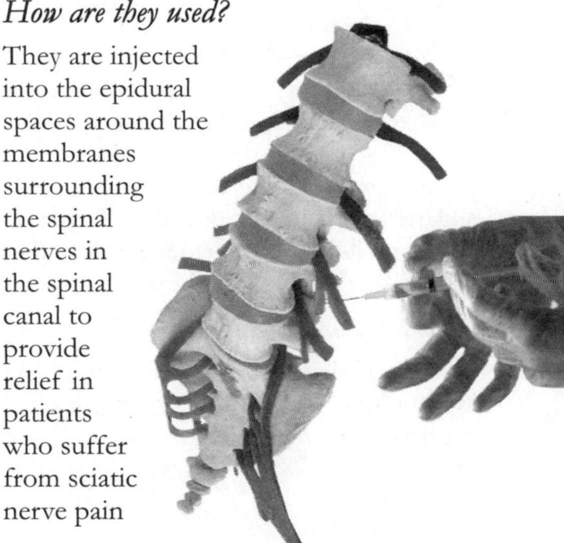

due to slipped disc. They can also be injected into the intervertebral joints to relieve inflammation, and can be given around ligaments and tendons to settle the pain and swelling at tender points in the spine.

A local anaesthetic may be injected with a Corticosteroid to relieve pain quickly. Often, this initial relief lasts for a few hours. It is commonly followed by a short period of slight worsening of the pain. The Corticosteroid usually begins to show its effect after a few days. The injection may be repeated for a more lasting relief.

Side effects

Side effects do not often occur with injected Corticosteroids; if they do, they are usually limited to the site of injection. These local side effects can include thinning of the skin or fat at the injection site, which may produce a dimple. Rarely, the area may get infected or inflammed.

Topical pain relievers

Several types of locally acting creams, ointments, gels and sprays are available to provide pain-relief. They contain a variety of chemicals, such as analgesics, locally acting numbing agents, and irritants, which work to ease the pain for short periods of time. Some of these preparations also reduce the inflammation.

Commonly used agents

Methylsalicylate, Diclofenac, Ibuprofen, Nimesulide, Capsicum, turpentine oil, eucalyptus oil, menthol, camphor and clove oil.

Mechanism of action

They act in various ways. While creams and gels that contain salicylates, Diclofenac, Ibuprofen, Nimesulide work as locally acting painkillers, Capsicum acts by depleting the nerve cells of a chemical called 'substance P' which is important for sending pain messages. Menthol, camphor and clove oil work as numbing agents. Counter-irritants act by improving the circulation to the area, and producing a barrage of mild neural sensations, which help to block the perception of pain from the deeper structures. They also produce warmth within the soft tissues.

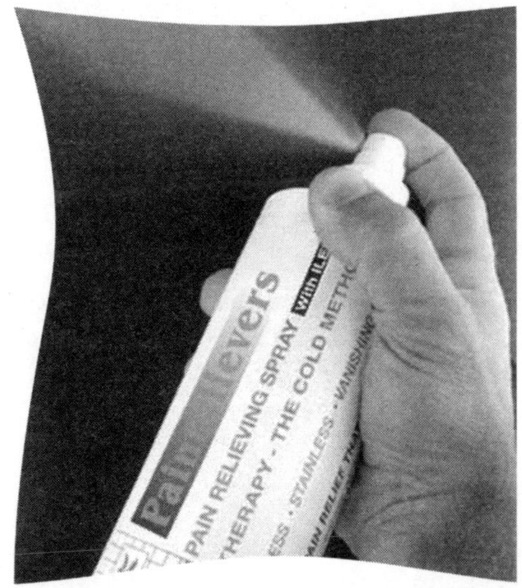

How are they used?

These locally acting agents are best rubbed gently on the painful areas of the back and are generally applied soon after a heat treatment. If the skin is broken, do not use them.

Side effects

They are quite safe and generally free of

side effects. But if they are wrongly applied on broken skin or wounds, they can prove toxic. Remember to wash your hands immediately after applying them and do not rub your eyes, since even a trace may irritate the eyes. If you develop a rash, discontinue their use.

12
Surgeries for
Bad Backs

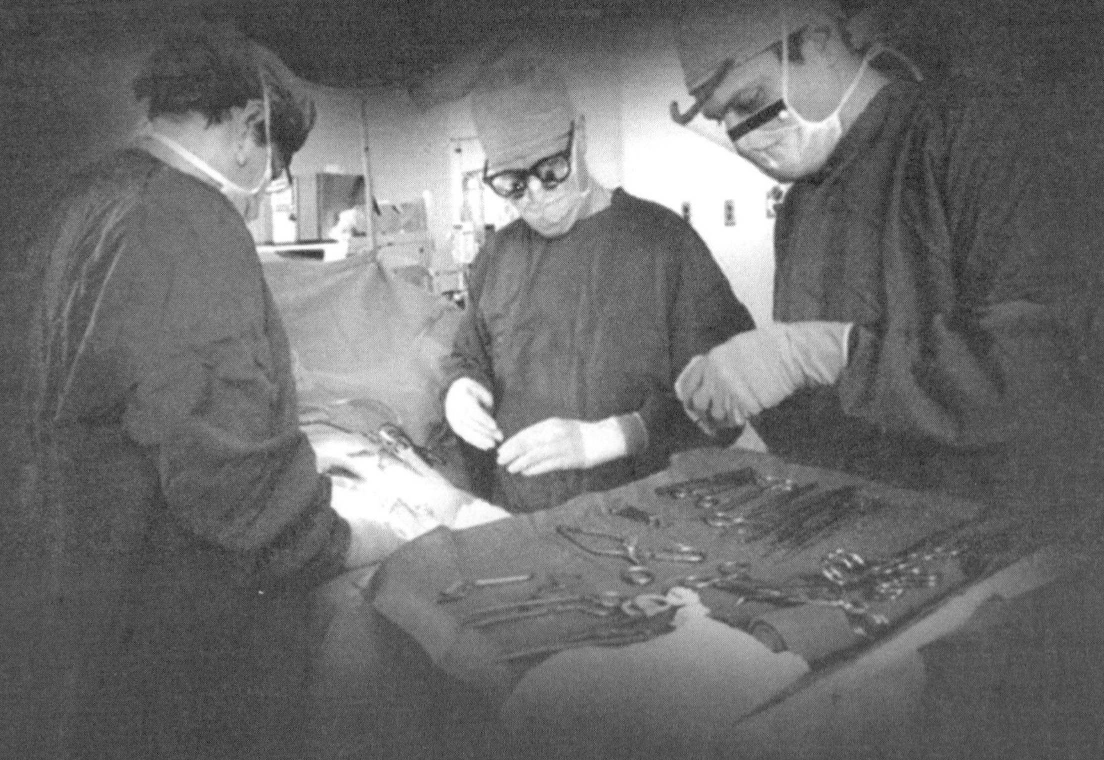

Spinal surgery is rarely the choice for bad backs. Only about one per cent people afflicted with common back pain go under the surgeon's knife. The simple truth is surgery does not offer any miraculous relief, nor it is a permanent cure in back pain patients. Without hesitation, except in a few rare acute situations when it may salvage the patient from permanent nerve damage, it is considered to hold very little merit and promise.

Despite the development of new techniques that offer quicker recovery and are much less invasive, this option must only be adopted if your doctor has a real good reason to wheel you into the operation room. You must discuss with him the benefits and compare them with the risk and cost of the surgery – the basic question being how much of an advantage would surgery hold over the other modes of treatment.

When to consider surgery

Spinal surgery is indicated on an emergency basis if a person develops sudden symptoms of *cauda equina* compression. Such an emergency can arise due to a large disc prolapse, leading to a sudden numbness in the seat area, loss of control over the urinary bladder or bowel, and loss of sensation and weakness of the toes or foot. Such patients may benefit from an immediate spinal surgery which may spare them of irreparable spinal nerve root damage.

Surgery may also be considered if a person has severe continuous pain due to a prolapsed disc pressing on a spinal nerve, or there's evidence of narrowing of the spinal canal (spinal stenosis) due to bony growths on the vertebrae, and when all other treatments have not benefited him or her.

Weigh the options carefully

Think carefully before you decide upon surgery. Talk to your doctor to find out what would be the benefit; how much improvement does he expect in the pain, pins and needles sensation, numbness, or muscular weakness; what would be the course of recovery; how long the relief will last; how much of an advantage would the operative procedure hold over the non-surgical treatment; and what would be the total cost of surgery.

You must clearly understand that the outcome of surgery is dictated by several factors – the damage that your back has incurred, the duration of your illness, the strength of your ligaments supporting your joints, the state of your bones and joints, your age, your weight and your ability to participate in the rehabilitation programme following surgery.

You must also carefully question your doctor of the risks that the surgery may hold, and the experience he has had with his patients so far. If you feel satisfied with his answers, go ahead, and don't look back. But if you feel unsure, do not hesitate to seek a second opinion before arriving at a decision. Given the latent risks and cost, it is advisable to talk to another doctor and know his viewpoint before you proceed with the operation.

Who should be your surgeon?

Spinal surgeries are carried out both by the orthopaedic surgeons and neurosurgeons. Your decision should be based on the training, experience, and expertise of the surgeon, and the recommendations of a friend, family member or personal physician who is familiar with the surgeon's work, availability, and bedside manners.

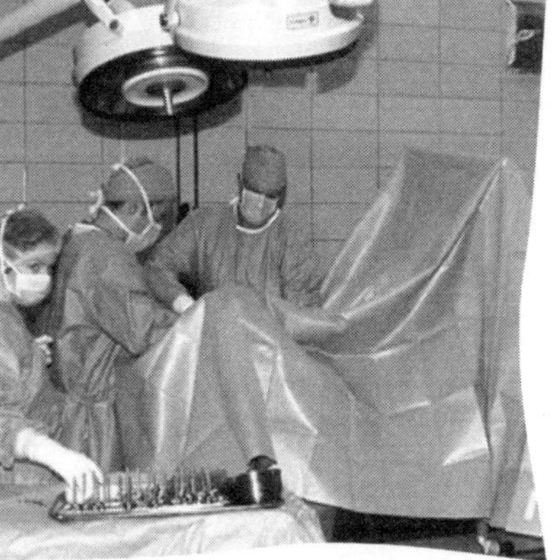

Choose the surgeon with care. A surgeon who is experienced and not rushed for time should have no hesitation in giving you time and explaining to you the procedure to be performed, the risks and benefits involved and the course of recovery. Let your family talk to him, express their expectation, and if you feel confident that he is the surgeon you can bank on, only then you should decide on getting operated by him.

Types of spinal surgeries

Surgeons perform a number of operative procedures to treat the back. The type of surgery is guided by the type of problem you have, your age and your overall health. While some surgeries are done to remove the pressure on spinal nerves and relieve pain by removing a displaced disc, some procedures focus on widening the spinal canal, and yet others help to stabilize the spine.

Taking a closer look at some of the commonly performed surgeries may help you understand how each surgery is useful in different clinical settings.

Surgery for slipped disc (discectomy)

When is discectomy done?

A slipped disc might sometimes press on a spinal nerve. If the problem is in the lower back, it is commonest between the fourth and fifth lumbar (L4-L5) vertebrae and fifth lumbar and first part of sacrum (L5-S1), it may cause sciatica. In the neck, the discs most commonly affected are those between the fifth and sixth cervical (C5-C6) vertebrae and the sixth and seventh cervical (C6-C7) vertebrae. If that is so, the pain and tingling travels to the arm, leading to a condition called brachialgia. In both cases, a discectomy would help remove that part of the disc that's protruding and compressing the nerve and provide relief.

When is discectomy a must?

If you develop acute symptoms of pressure on nerve roots with loss of sensation or function, or feel weak in a limb, and the surgeon feels that the situation is correctable by surgery, do not wait; just go ahead.

If the situation is not that desperate, and you simply have a sciatic pain or brachialgia, work on the principle that if you try hard enough, non-surgical treatment regimen will definitely benefit you and you may not require surgery. But if despite giving a fair trial, these non-surgical measures fail, the pain is so severe that it does not let you rest or sleep, is recurrent and hampers your normal life, you may think of surgery.

How is it done?

Once the patient goes under, the surgeon makes an incision to expose the ligaments that cover the spine. He then carefully dissects the ligaments and exposes the nerves within the spinal canal, and also the vertebrae. On locating the prolapsed disc, he removes its protruding portion, leaving the main body of the disc intact. Next, he checks if the nerve he has freed can move easily. If the nerve is impeded in any way, the surgeon removes tiny pieces of bone from the vertebrae to ease its passage. Finally, he stitches back the ligaments, muscle and skin.

Newer ways of doing disc surgery

In recent years, major advances have taken place in the field of spinal surgery. Newer, less-invasive technologies are being developed for the benefit of the patients. While these techniques help fasten the pace of recovery and also hold some small added advantages over the traditional disc surgery, they are much more expensive than the older surgery. You may decide in their favour only if you think the benefits deserve the extra cost, and if you have the ability to pay.

Micro discectomy

Today, an increasing number of disc surgeries are being done with the newer microsurgical technique. The biggest advantage of the procedure is that it requires a very small incision, no more than 2.5 cm (one-inch) long, and the surgeon carries out the entire surgery through this opening, using an operating microscope and specially designed microsurgical instruments. Consequently, the disruption and damage to the bones, muscles, ligaments and other tissues is much less and the recovery is much faster. The patient may be sent home walking by the same evening or the next day.

Endoscopic discectomy

Endoscopic discectomy is the newest keyhole surgery done for disc removal. It uses a specialized endoscope, which is introduced through a ½ or 1 cm opening in the back. The surgeon expertly pushes specially designed endoscopic instruments through separate keyhole incisions into the operative area to help complete his job. The extremely fine and delicate movements of the surgical instruments are performed under the guidance of a TV screen that transmits live pictures through an attached camera on the eyepiece of the endoscope. Again, the major benefit of this technique is a much faster recovery.

Follow-up

Following the operation you will be encouraged to get up and move about after the first couple of days. You may have to wear a lumbar support for the first few weeks.

Most people recover well from the operation and can return to work within a few months. Those who have developed loss of sensation or have lost muscle power generally get better over time. An active rehabilitation plan is drawn keeping pace with the progress. The pace of recovery is fastest during the first three months, but the best results are visible by the end of the first year.

Decompression of the spinal canal

When is spinal decompression surgery done?

This surgery is done to enlarge a narrow spinal canal and ease the compression of the spinal cord or spinal nerve(s), thus, freeing the person from the pressure symptoms. The surgery may be of use in a number of situations. Most commonly, it is done for patients with advanced spondylosis who have big bony outgrowths (osteophytes) growing into the gaps between the vertebrae or into the spinal canal. The surgery may also benefit people with spondylolisthesis, a condition where a vertebral arch breaks off the vertebral body causing the vertebra to slip out of line and press on a nerve root or the spinal cord, resulting in severe pain.

How is it done?

Once the patient is under general anaesthesia, the surgeon makes an incision on the back. He dissects carefully until he reaches the posterior elements and the spines of the vertebrae. Next, he removes pieces of the vertebral bone to relieve the pressure on the spinal cord or nerve roots. A number of variations of this technique are practiced, but the principle essentially is the same.

Follow-up

Recovery from a decompression surgery is generally quite uncomplicated. The operated person can return to normal activities, including work, within a few months of the operation.

Spinal fusion

When is spinal fusion done?

This procedure is usually performed to stabilize and stiffen a painful arthritic spine. This may be necessary when the intervertebral joints are diseased and slip out of alignment, or to prevent problems such as spondylolisthesis from increasing. It can also be used to stabilize the lower spine if parts of it move too much when you bend over. This problem, known as lumbar instability, can result in back pain and frequent bouts of sciatica. However, this surgery is only done when there is no other choice, since the section of the spine fused during the operation remains permanently rigid and unbending.

How is it done?

The operation involves taking strips of bone from another part of the body, usually the hip-bone, and grafting them vertically across two or three vertebrae. Alternatively, one or more discs are removed and the empty space packed with tiny pieces of bone, which fuse with the vertebrae above and below, locking that part of the spine rigid.

The surgery can be done in two different ways: the anterior approach, whereby the surgeon, instead of going through the weak posterior area of the back, accesses the spine via the front. This is a more difficult surgery, since it requires the surgeon to go via the chest or abdomen. Once the instable area is reached, the surgeon removes the inter- vertebral discs and fuses the vertebrae. The procedure is called anterior spinal fusion.

Fact file

Dr Russell Hibbs of the New York Orthopaedic Hospital pioneered the surgery of spinal fusion in 1911. The surgery came to be a blessing for patients with tuberculosis of the spine. It helped check the worsening hunchback deformity. Alas, the Hunchback of Notre Dam never benefited from the surgery.

The Hong Kong operation was developed by Professor Arthur Hodgeson and Dr Frances Stodge in the 1950s. The first report about the new technique was published in the *British Journal of Surgery* in 1956. The surgery was evolved to treat tuberculosis of the spine, and entailed approaching the diseased spine from the abdominal cavity or chest, removing the pus, unhealthy tissues and diseased bone under direct vision, and filling up the gaps with healthy bone grafts obtained from the adjoining ribs and hip-bone.

Dr Paul Harrington (1911-1980) an orthopaedic surgeon from Kansas, USA, was the first to introduce engineering principles into medicine. He invented stainless steel surgical implants that are still in use today, nearly fifty years after he first used them. He also developed the steel implants to straighten a twisted spine and the posterior spinal-fusion technique to treat spinal deformity.

Most surgeons however prefer doing the simpler posterior spinal fusion, where the surgeon accesses the weak area through an incision in the back. This procedure is usually performed on patients with chronic back pain who suffer from spinal canal stenosis, with degenerative discs and extensive arthritis of intervertebral joints. A posterior spinal fusion of the vertebrae above and below is done using bone grafts taken from the hip-bone. Until the bone grafts get integrated, a brace has to be worn to limit the movements of the back.

How does the hip-bone behave after grafts are taken from it?

Taking bone pieces from the hip-bone has no lasting ill effects, but the area does remain tender for some weeks.

Follow-up

Following the surgery, the patient is usually allowed to get out of bed after a couple of weeks. But he or she must wear a corset for about six weeks.

Spinal fusion leaves the back greatly weakened and recovery can easily take up a year. As soon as you get better, it is time to begin working with a physiotherapist to regain as much strength and flexibility as possible.

13 Alternative Therapies

What should we do about events which, by all rules, ought not to occur, but which nevertheless occur? One option: we can shut our eyes to the queer embarrassing data, in the hope that if we don't look at them, they will go away and leave us in peace. Alternatively, we can accept them, for the time being as inexplicable anomalies, while doing our best to modify current theory in such a way that it will 'save the appearances'.

From telepathy to acupuncture, queer facts get ignored by the very people whose business it is to investigate them – get ignored because they fail to fit into any of the academic pigeonholes and do not suffer themselves to be explained in terms of accredited theories.

–Aldous Huxley

If you are a sufferer of frequent attacks of severe back pain, you may have thought about using alternative treatment systems on several occasions. You may have even consulted and taken treatment of an *ayurvedacharya*, acupuncturist, aromatherapist, homeopath, naturopath, masseur, osteopath, or yoga teacher. Else you may have found relief through alternative therapy, but feel unsure if switching on to an unorthodox treatment system is sensible in this modern scientific age. It is also possible you feel somewhat embarrassed at doing so and feel uncertain if you should confide in your primary doctor.

Frankly, if you have benefited from any of these treatments, that's the best barometer of their worth. Just make sure that what's being done is harmless, does not use any natural or man-made substances that may damage your body, and that you are not being taken for a ride, duped of money or being cheated by being given modern medicines in the guise of a *desi* packet. If you are sure of these facts, you may be best off by continuing the relief-providing therapy. In fact, do not be embarrassed in sharing the fact with your doctor, unless he or she believes in living in an academic pigeonhole.

Even though this chapter is neither substantiation nor a censure of the several existent alternative therapies, it offers a window so that you do not feel it's wrong to use them even while you find relief. The authors make no claim to be truly knowledgeable about the alternative systems, but feel indulgent enough to share the basics. The fact is, many of these systems have been in existence for thousands of years and have survived despite the advances in modern medicine. If so, they must certainly hold some benefit. Yet, since they haven't been tested using mainstream scientific methods, it's difficult to pronounce any verdict on their effectiveness or safety and it is harder still to endorse or negate them.

It is possible that just as several folk remedies have been integrated into modern medicine, many of the practices of traditional medicine may also have found their way into the therapeutic fold of current medical treatment. Take, for instance, yogic exercises: many of them could easily be the forerunner of modern-day physiotherapy.

The best course may be to amalgamate the good of all systems, and develop a holistic therapeutic approach. Mainstream scientific methods can easily be tailored to evaluate the effectiveness and safety of these systems, provided the participants are prepared to seek the truth.

Ayurveda

Ayurveda means the 'science of life'. A holistic medical system that dates back to 1500 BC, it is man's journey through the ages. Ayurveda embodies man's accumulated wisdom of medical practice and knowledge and offers surprisingly detailed information on a variety of diseases, including their aetiology, inheritance and regimens to treat them. Within its tomes, there is a description of a number of remedies, mostly based on herbs and metal ions. The philosophy is rather complex and difficult to translate into modern scientific terms.

Ayurveda views the human being in totality, rather than at the micro or molecular level. It believes that if a person is aware of his or her basic constitution, he or she can take action, change diet, behaviour and emotional response and achieve equilibrium with the self to live a balanced and healthy life.

The basic principle

Ayurveda believes that all organic or inorganic substances consist of five basic elements: space (ether), air, fire, water, and earth. The active, or energized, forms of these elements make three main types of energy or *doshas*. They are called *vata, pitta* and *kapha*.

- Air and space give rise to *vata,* the energy of movement.
- Fire and water generate *pitta*, the energy of digestion and metabolism.
- Water and earth produce *kapha*, the energy that shapes the body and binds the billions of cells in the body together.

Each person is a unique combination of *vata, pitta* and *kapha*. In some individuals, one *dosha* rules; in others, two *doshas* rule; and in few, all three *doshas* are equally balanced.

The balance of *doshas* determines an individual's constitution. All diseases relate to the imbalance of *doshas*. Each *dosha* is said to have a 'seat' organ in the body, which has the ability to absorb and eliminate small imbalances of *dosha*. Balancing the *doshas* is critical to good health, and the main thrust of ayurveda focuses on this balance.

A person can broadly be categorized under the following types:

Vata types

Built and disposition: Slight-built, may be tall or short, dry skin and hair; creative, with impulsive nervous movements and tends to waste energy.
Dominant element: air, then ether.
Organ seat: colon.
Tastes that stimulate *vata:* pungent, bitter, astringent.
Tastes that calm *vata:* sweet, sour, and salty.
***Vata* seasons**: autumn and early winter.
Foods that calm excess *vata:* carrots; cooked root vegetables; and moist, warming foods.

Pitta types

Built and disposition: Evenly proportioned and of average height. Confident and ambitious, hence aggressively competitive.
Dominant element: fire, then water.
Organ seats: stomach and small intestine.
Tastes that increase *pitta:* sour, salty,

pungent; *pitta* types should limit red meat.
Tastes that calm excess *pitta:* sweet, astringent, and bitter.
***Pitta* season**: summer.
Foods that calm excess *pitta:* cooling foods, especially gourd juice, grass juice, cucumber, and salads.

Kapha types

Built and disposition: Robust built, physically strong, oily skin and slow moving. Stable and patient, they are inclined to be possessive.
Dominant element: water, then earth.
Organ seat of *kapha:* stomach and lungs.
Foods that increase *kapha:* milk and dairy products.
Tastes that increase *kapha:* sweet, sour and salty.
Tastes that calm excess *kapha:* pungent, bitter, and astringent.
***Kapha* season**: middle of winter.

Foods that calm excess *kapha:* apples, pears, hot foods, leafy vegetables, beans and lentils.

Diagnosis

Practitioners of ayurveda primarily rely on the clinical history and physical examination of the patient to come to a diagnosis. The clinical interview includes detailed questions about personal and family history, lifestyle, eating habits, digestion and individual's interpersonal relationships. Physical examination mainly rests on reading the pulse of the patient. The pulse is read at three points on both the wrists (to correspond with the three *doshas*). Most *ayurvedacharyas* prefer to examine the patient in a fasting state, because of the belief that food may affect the pulse.

Ayurvedic texts describe many forms of arthritis. Most are stated to be born of *vata* disorders, some due to genetic causes, and interestingly, some are said to be associated with sexually transmitted illnesses. These concepts do not seem alien in today's state of knowledge, with several forms of arthritis being taken as genetic disorders and arthritis being a known component in some of the sexually transmitted diseases.

Treatment

The treatment regimen is guided by the diagnosis. In general, it always calls for some change in diet. You will be advised to eat certain foods and shun others since they may exacerbate the disease. In addition, you may also perhaps be advised to change the timing of the meals, depending on your *dosha* and the season of the year. To neutralize the doshic imbalance, a cooling *(shaman)* regimen is prescribed, and you may be given a unique set of herbs or minerals.

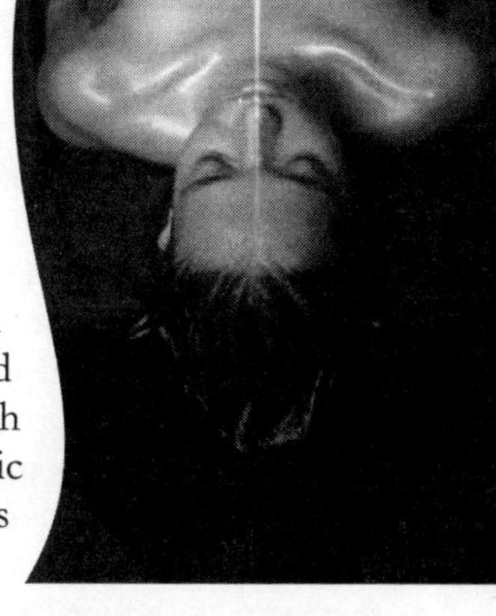

You may also be required to undergo a cleansing and detoxification programme, called *shodan*, which includes: therapeutic enemas, purgatives (including the herbal remedy, Triphala), saunas, massage with oils, foot massage and washing out the nasal passages jointly termed as *panchakarma*.

This aims at purification of the body and blood. After the cleansing process is complete, you go into a programme of rejuvenation. Specific herbs, meditation and sunbathing form the basis of this energizing regimen called *rasayana.*

Ayurvedic remedies

Consisting of herbs, minerals and vegetables, each prescription varies according to the external environment, season, *dosha* type and *dosha* imbalance. Sometimes a carrier, such as water, honey or *ghee* (clarified butter) is used to formulate compound formulas.

Interestingly, some of the ayurveda herbs have also won the sanction of modern research. Thus, *Boswellia serrata* has been found to be useful in relief of arthritis symptoms, while an external cream made up of cayenne offers respite in osteoarthritis. The anti-inflammatory properties of turmeric have also been substantiated. The long list of arthritis remedies in ayurveda is not just limited to herbs; it also includes metals such as gold, silver and mercury-based preparations.

Acupuncture

An ancient medical treatment that originated in China, acupuncture involves inserting thin needles under your skin. The concept is that needles stimulate specific points that allow the free flow of *chi*, the Chinese word for energy or life force. Traditional acupuncturists believe that pain is reduced and health is restored when *chi* flows without obstruction along pathways called meridians that run throughout the body.

During a typical session, an acupuncturist inserts anywhere from one to 30 metal needles for 15 to 30 minutes. The acupuncturist also may manipulate the needles manually or by electrical stimulation. Some modern acupuncturists also use a laser beam to stimulate the

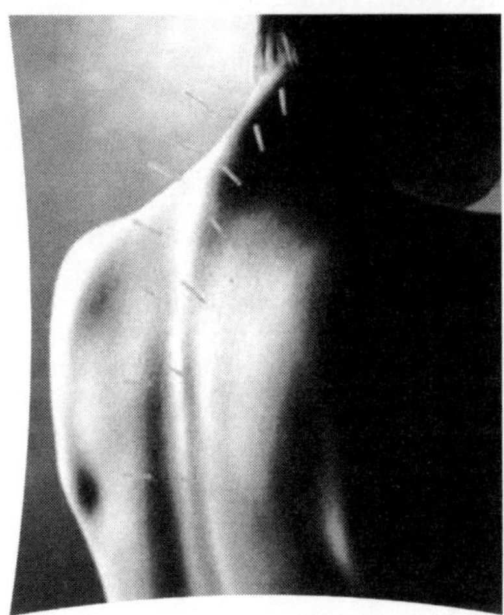

obstructed points. The frequency and number of treatment sessions are guided by the symptoms and the acupuncturist's personal preference.

Scientific research indicates that acupuncture stimulates the body's own immune system and generates morphine-like painkilling chemicals, called endorphins in the brain. For this reason, acupuncture particularly appeals to people who cannot tolerate side effects associated with long-term use of non-steroidal anti-inflammatory drugs (NSAIDs).

Acupuncture is generally a low-risk treatment. However, you must find a skilled practitioner who uses sterile needles or laser for giving therapy. Several modern hospitals in India offer the facility of acupuncture as a part of their service.

Aromatherapy

If you don't mind being clubbed in the same class as the Moghul royalty, try this ancient form of healing. Aromatherapy uses oils derived from plant extracts and resins to promote both health and beauty. Its practitioners believe these oils can help treat various illnesses, including back pain and inflammation, when massaged into the skin or inhaled.

Modern medical experts admit that therapeutic massage can help relieve muscle pain and stiffness and promote relaxation. Although it is true that many modern medicines are derived from plant extracts, more study is needed to determine whether any medicinal benefits are associated with the plant oils used in aromatherapy.

In any case, if you do not mind the expense, and find the treatment beneficial, it could do no harm. The 'feel good' factor is most certainly a rejuvenator. Several spa centres in India offer the facility of aromatherapy.

Grandma's concoctions

While the scientific basis of these concoctions is hard to obtain, the elders in the community have preserved the following treatment recipes for back pain for a long time:

Massage with garlic juice: Slowly heat 10 cloves of garlic in 60 ml of mustard, sesame or coconut oil, till the mix turns to a light brown hue. Apply the preparation three or four times daily over the sore area of the back. Continue for at least the next 15 days.

Potato poultice: Make a soft moist mass of potato. Heat it, spread on cloth, and apply to the aching part of the back.

Fenugreek (methi) *seeds*: A daily intake of 25-50 gram of fenugreek seeds divided equally and taken with morning supper and dinner (approximately two teaspoons with each meal) are considered to be most useful for elimination of pain and swelling in arthritis and back pain.

Lemon juice: Some people recommend vitamin-C-rich lemon juice twice a day.

You may try, but there is no guarantee that the recipes will deliver.

Homeopathy

Practiced all around the globe today, homeopathy was born in Germany in the late 18th century. Extremely popular in India due to its low cost and presumed safety, its practice is governed by the 'law of similars', a principle given by German physician Samuel Hahnemann.

The philosophy is simple: if a substance causes you to develop certain symptoms when you are healthy, a small dose of this substance can treat illnesses with similar symptoms.

Homeopaths believe they have remedies for most difficult cases of backache. A number of pills in *Materia Medica* lay claim to cures for back pain. The diagnosis in homeopathy is entirely based on symptoms. During an evaluation, a homeopath may ask questions about your physical, mental and emotional symptoms before prescribing the treatment. Most homeopathic treatments are extremely diluted preparations of natural substances, such as plants and minerals.

Scientific research has not yet explained how homeopathic medicines work. Since most homeopathic medicines are so diluted, they contain virtually no molecules of the active substances, many modern scientists are sceptical about their effectiveness. Yet, some experimental work suggests that there may be more to it than meets the eye. Molecular memory is just one of the many possibilities.

The biggest limitation with homeopathy however is that most homeopaths hate to divulge their prescriptions and wish to keep them a complete secret. This needs to change.

Manual manipulation

The practice of chiropractic was founded in 1895 at Davenport, Iowa, by Canadian-American healer Daniel David Palmer, who developed a system of manually manipulating the joints, especially the spine. A more *desi* version of the practice has existed in India probably since much longer. Call them osteopaths, bonesetters or joint setters, they are a legend in the countryside.

Chiropractics and osteopaths manipulate the back to restore the alignment of the spinal joints. The practice is so lucrative that some medical practitioners also employ these manoeuvres with varying degrees of success and treat people of backache.

The real life story

Fifty-year-old Harbans Kaur, a bank manager and a patient of one of the authors, has this most extraordinary story to tell. She had suffered a slipped disc some twenty years ago. Having been through the rigours of treatment without any relief, she finally decided to brave a disc surgery rather than suffer. On the day of surgery, all set, she was waiting for her turn in the pre-op ward. A young child lay on the adjoining bed. The child blissfully dosed off, and lying precariously near the edge was about to fall. Harbans, gaping in horror, and fearing the worst, suddenly sprang up to catch the child just as the child was about to topple over. As she did so, she felt something click in her back and snap into position. But what a pleasant surprise: her back symptoms had also totally disappeared. She was discharged on the same day, without having to undergo the surgery.

Osteopaths, chiropractors, physiotherapists and fitness therapists, all practice this system. They may or may not be qualified to practice, and many orthopaedic surgeons feel that chiropractic is not scientific. In some people, there have been reports of spinal column coming to harm by osteopathic manipulation, but many more patients swear to its effectiveness.

Clearly, the art of spinal manipulation merits a careful study. It calls for knowledge, expert hands, skill, and experience, but if the practitioner knows the job, it may work well as a simple, inexpensive, no-nonsense and low-tech treatment. However, the good doctor must know when not to manipulate a spine.

Massage therapy

Massage is a popular ancient form of treatment. Using a variety of mineral oils and lubricants, trained masseurs employ smooth rubbing strokes and kneading movements to help stretch out tight muscles, taut tendons, stiff joints and relieve the body of stress and pain. If done in the correct manner, it can prove useful in managing chronic back pain. The key is no vigorous rub of the tender area and no painful stretching of the damaged tendons or muscles.

Several theories prevail on how massage works. While one states that massage promotes capillary, venous and lymphatic flow in stiff or tight tissues, the other propounds that it works by removing the toxic wastes like lactic acid and carbon dioxide from the affected region and encouraging the flow of fresh oxygenated blood and nutrients into the area. Claims have also been made that it stimulates the release of endorphins, which act like morphine and provide relief from pain.

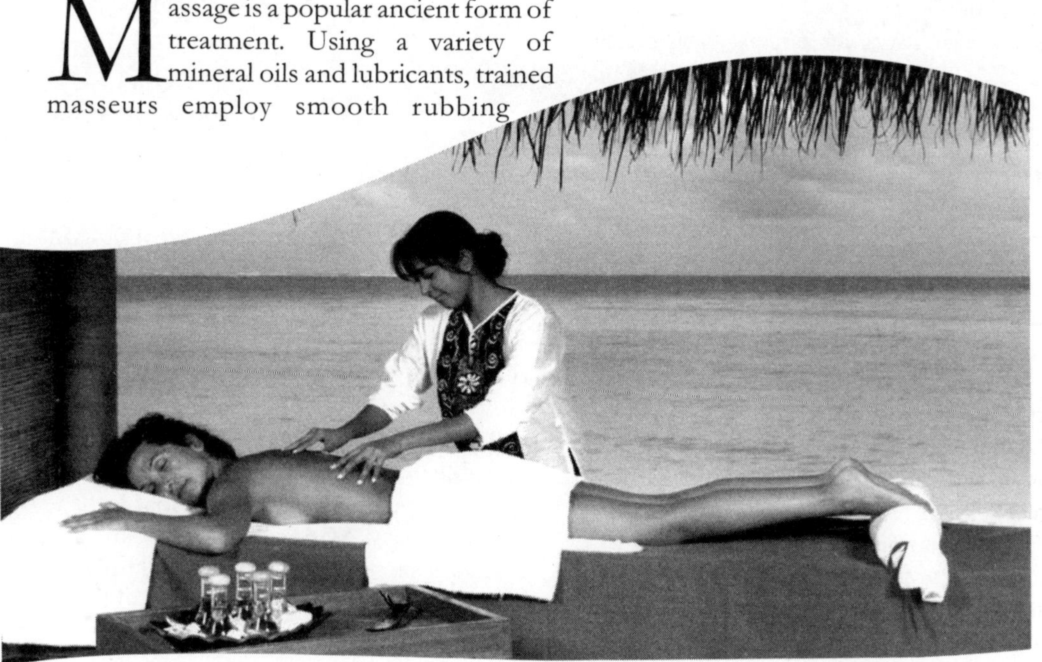

Massage in ancient times

Massage therapy using herbal oils has been widely practiced in Hindu medicine since 1500 BC. The practice is still popular in combination with herbal medicine and fasting, in the belief that most physical problems, including arthritis, arise from digestive disorders.

Hippocrates (460-380 BC) has also described several massage manoeuvres for pain relief. It is surprising to learn that though it was not known at that time that blood flows from and to the heart, he had described how massage is effective only if strokes are made along the limbs, away from the feet and hands and towards the heart. Among later proponents, Ambroise Pares, the great French physician, popularised massage, and Queen Victoria who suffered from arthritis, was also a great protagonist of the massage therapy.

Both Hindu and Chinese medicine employ a combined spiritual, mental and physical approach to pain treatment in the belief that an unhealthy, stressful and undisciplined life forms the basis of pain and arthritis. Massage therapy is therefore performed in a clean tranquil environment, away from pollution. A background of soothing music has a calming effect on the senses. All of these provide an overall positive effect when combined with massage therapy.

The 18th century British navigator and explorer, Captain James Cook, who commanded three major voyages of discovery, charting and naming many islands of the Pacific Ocean, has logged in his travel reminiscences the event of his receiving a successful massage treatment at the hands of a Polynesian family during an acute episode of sciatica pain.

Nutritional supplements

Glucosamine and chondroitin sulphate are dietary supplements that have recently gained favour as therapy for osteoarthritis. Found naturally in the human body, Glucosamine is incorporated into substances that give cartilage its strength and rigidity, such as Chondroitin, which helps cartilage attract and retain water.

There is some evidence that Glucosamine and chondroitin sulphate supplements may help maintain existing cartilage and stimulate growth of new cartilage. But large, long-term studies are needed to ratify whether these supplements offer any lasting benefit.

New claims for vitamins, minerals and dietary supplements are also in the news almost every day. Vitamins A, C and E, called antioxidants, are being studied as a possible treatment of arthritis because they may help prevent cell damage that leads to joint pain. Minerals like calcium, manganese, magnesium, selenium and boron also are included in the good health preparations.

Soybean and avocado oils also are being researched as a possible treatment of osteoarthritis. Other dietary supplements derived from sources such as algae and bacteria found in yoghurt are also part of the growing array of potential complementary therapies.

Transcutaneous nerve stimulation

Known since before Christ, Greeks and Romans of the olden times employed several weird methods to stimulate a nerve to produce analgesic effect and treat lumbago. Aristotle used sting rays, while the later-day Romans used electric eels and torpedo rays. In the 18th century, Benjamin Franklin introduced the electric shock machine in hospitals, and later a French physician, Sarlandiere, developed an electro-acupuncture device for the treatment of rheumatic pains.

The same thought is reflected in the modern-day transcutaneous electric nerve stimulation (TENS) devices. The therapist sends mild electric currents through electrodes attached to the patient's skin. The principle is simple. The tiny amounts of electric current to areas around the pain site stimulates the nerve endings in the skin and the signals from these override the pain messages being sent from the deeper structures, such as inflamed joints of the back to the brain.

TENS do-it-yourself home devices are also available. They can be used to relieve chronic back pain. You just switch on the stimulator, and the device is active. However, the benefit of TENS is variable.

Yoga and yogic asanas

Yoga is a way of life. Derived from Sanskrit, the word yoga signifies the 'union of inner self with the eternal soul'. The ancients developed the system as a means of achieving harmony in relation to the inner self and the environment.

If you can practise yoga, you could easily prevent back trouble and most other lifestyle disorders. A branch of yoga called *hathayoga* focuses on special yogic postures or *asanas*. Unlike other exercise systems, *hathayoga* favours simultaneous relaxation, whereby movements related to breathing and posture blend into each other. Some *asanas* may be of special significance in prevention of back pain.

The asanas

Bhujanga asana (the serpent pose)

Lie down straight on your stomach (chest down). Keep the legs straight. Let the feet touch each other. The soles of the feet

should face upwards. Keep the hands on the sides of the chest. Raise the head and stretch it back, pushing your tongue out. Raise the chest slowly. Give a backward bend to the back as much as possible, while keeping the waist and the legs in contact with the floor. Experience a steady pull along the back, from the neck downwards. Draw a deep breath once you achieve this position. Maintain the position for five counts, lower the chest and relax the backbone. As you return the chest to its resting position, exhale slowly for a count of five. After brief relaxation, repeat the drill. Repeat each movement five times.

Pawan mukta asana (the half-embryo pose)

Lie down straight on the back facing the ceiling. Keep both hands by the side. Bend one knee towards the chest. Hold the leg with both hands holding the knee. Pull the knee towards the chest, and keep the position for five counts. Release the knee, and straighten the leg. Rest for five counts

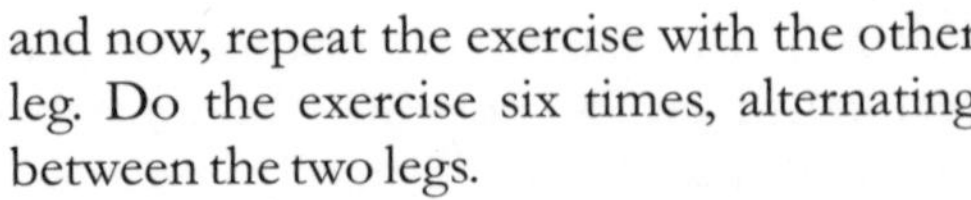

and now, repeat the exercise with the other leg. Do the exercise six times, alternating between the two legs.

Shalabh asana (the locust pose)

Lie down straight on your stomach with chin touching the floor. Keep your hands on the sides of the body, with fingers straight and touching each other. Take a

deep breath, and raise your right leg slowly, without a jerk. Maintain the position for half a minute at first and gradually increase the holding time. Return to original position, relax and repeat with the left leg. Next, raise both the legs together. Do it only twice at first.

Setubandha asana (the bridge pose)

Lie down straight on the back, facing the ceiling. Keep both hands by the side. Bend your knees, drawing the heels towards the buttocks. Both knees and both heels should approximate each other. Lift the hips and the trunk, while keeping the shoulders and feet on the floor. Once the hips are raised, support them with your palms. Use the hands to help raise the hips further, as high as possible without straining yourself.

Breathe normally, and maintain this position for five counts. Slowly return to the original

position. Rest for two or three normal breaths. Repeat five times.

Ekpada uttan asana (the single leg lifting pose)

Lie down straight on your back, facing the ceiling. Keep the heels together and both

arms straight alongside your body. Inhale slowly and deeply and hold your breath. Stretch out one leg and toe, and lift the leg straight towards the sky, about 10-12 inches from the floor. Maintain this position for five counts, while holding your breath. Start exhaling as the leg is lowered to the floor. Rest for five counts. Repeat six times while alternating between the two legs.

After some practice, the leg can be raised higher and brought into a perpendicular position. Be careful, however, not to strain.

Shavasana (the dead man's pose)

Lie down on your back with the hands by the side. Breathe easy. Keep the eyes closed. Feel the whole body go still.

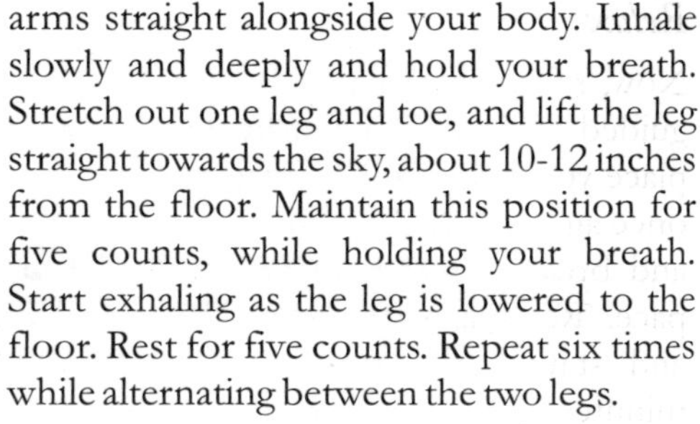

Without opening your eyes, draw your mental attention to the toes. See through your mind that the toes are relaxed. Then slowly move upward…checking if the knees, thighs, waist, spine, shoulders, neck, arms, palms, fingers and the rest of the anatomical areas are relaxed. Rotate your head a little by first turning left and then right. Let the head now rest in a relaxed position. Now your entire body is relaxed.

Relax

Now, relax your mind. Use visualization or guided imagery. Think of being in a beautiful place you have visited. Imagine you're there once again. Relax, breathe deeply. Breathe in and breathe out 10-12 times at a leisurely pace. Relax as if you are about to sleep, and stay in this position for about five minutes.

Pranayama (the breathing technique)

Pranayama is the yoga of breathing. It has three stages: exhalation, inhalation, and retention of breath. The technique is simple. Sit on the ground in lotus or easy pose. Hold the spine, neck and head absolutely upright. Look straight. Stretch your arms and rest your wrists on the knees. Bring your thumb and index finger in apposition so that they form a circle. Keep the other three fingers straight. Breathe normally.

Now, exhale slowly through both nostrils and at the same time, contract your abdominal muscles to expel the air from the lungs. Pause for a second. Next, inhale as deep as you can, sucking air through the nose, and letting it fill all the vessels in the body. Let the abdominal muscles also expand. Pause for a second. Exhale. Repeat 10 or 15 times.

Dhayana (meditation)

Dhayana or meditation is a relaxed state of consciousness. It is a technique that helps you enter a deeply restful state, and calms your nervous system and bodily functions.

There are several ways to meditate, but the simplest approach is to sit quietly and focus on nothing or on your breathing or on a *mantra* – a simple sound repeated over and over.

Regular practice of meditation can relax your breathing, slow brain waves and decrease the muscle tension and heart rate. It also can lessen your body's response to the chemicals it produces when you are stressed by pain.

The yogic way of life

Yoga is not only about doing *asanas*, but it also inculcates a healthy balanced diet, a lifestyle which allows no harmful habits like smoking or alcohol, regular stress-free routine, mental calmness and emotional stability. Practise yoga regularly, and you may counter the effects of ageing, ease stress or tension and improve posture, movement and balance.If you feel tempted, you can start now.

PART FIVE

Less Common Causes of Backache

Backache can be a part and parcel of a variety of conditions. While some people suffer a break and slippage in the bony pieces of their back armature, others may find their sacro-iliac joints that join the bottom pieces of their spine to the pelvis strained, inflamed, or jammed. Then again, tuberculosis might strike the vertebral bodies causing breakdown and collapse of the bones, and the loss of discs.

Some young people, mostly men and rarely women, suffer a bent-back deformity due to a crippling condition, called ankylosing spondylitis or bamboo spine. Weakened osteoporotic vertebral bones can also collapse and cause severe backache. Equally, you

could suffer back pain due to stress seeping into your back muscles – a condition that goes by the name of fibromyalgia.

The saga of back pain does not end here. What you might think of as a back trouble may occasionally be an altogether different problem: a stone in the kidney or ureter, urinary infection, swollen pancreas, a patch of pneumonia, pleurisy, reproductive tract infections, or a heart attack.

This section focuses on some of these assorted conditions that can cause back pain, and offers practical advice on how to win over them.

14

All about Spinal Break and Slippage

Spondylolysis and Spondylolisthesis

You may find this hard to believe, but many people hide a break in their backbone. The ring-like arch of a vertebral body is split open. This break is either due to a birth defect; a fracture suffered in the growing years; or less often, a part of the ageing process. This condition is called spondylolysis. It usually affects the

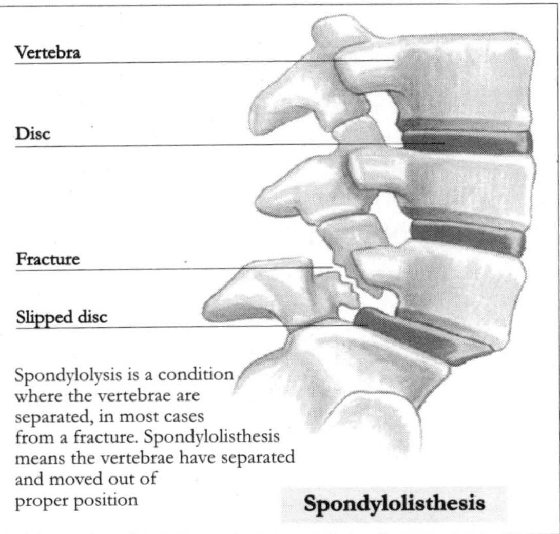

Spondylolysis is a condition where the vertebrae are separated, in most cases from a fracture. Spondylolisthesis means the vertebrae have separated and moved out of proper position

Spondylolisthesis

fifth lumbar vertebra in the lower back, and much less commonly, the fourth lumbar vertebra.

A person who has this defect can suffer further damage. The vertebra, unable to maintain its proper position, can start to shift out of place. This condition is called spondylolisthesis. If too much slippage occurs, the bones may begin to press on nerves and surgery may be necessary to correct the condition.

Risk factors

Some people are born with a break or gap in a vertebral ring. This vertebra is therefore vulnerable to slip forward in relation to the rest of the bones of the spinal column. Significant periods of rapid skeletal growth may encourage this slippage.

Yet, in many young people, the problem is born out of such sports as gymnastics, weightlifting and football, which put a great deal of stress on the bones in the lower back. They also require that the athlete constantly over-stretch (hyperextend) the spine. In either case, the result is a stress fracture on one or both sides of the vertebra.

Some people may also acquire the defect following a back injury, such as the impact of falling off a ladder and landing on the feet. Others suffer due to the wear-and-tear of daily life, and a few due to a tumour that eats away this part of the vertebral bone.

Symptoms

Many people with spondylolysis and spondylolisthesis have no symptoms, and only come to know of the problem when it is revealed on an X-ray done for a different problem. In others, life may be plagued with several difficulties. They may suffer from pain in the low back, especially after exercise, an increased swayback, and tight hamstrings, resulting in changes in posture and walk. If the slippage is significant, the bones may narrow the spinal canal and begin to compress the spinal nerve roots.

This causes pain and/or weakness in one or both thighs and legs, and may reduce ability to control bowel and bladder function.

Diagnostic tests

The defect or break in the vertebral arch can be diagnosed on the X-rays of the lower back (lumbo-sacral spine). The *pars interarticularis*, or the portion between the upper and lower articular processes of a lumbar vertebra shows a crack or fracture. This condition is called spondylolysis. The X-ray confirms the bony abnormality.

If the gap at the pars widens, the lumbar vertebra tends to shift forward in relation to the rest of the spine. The

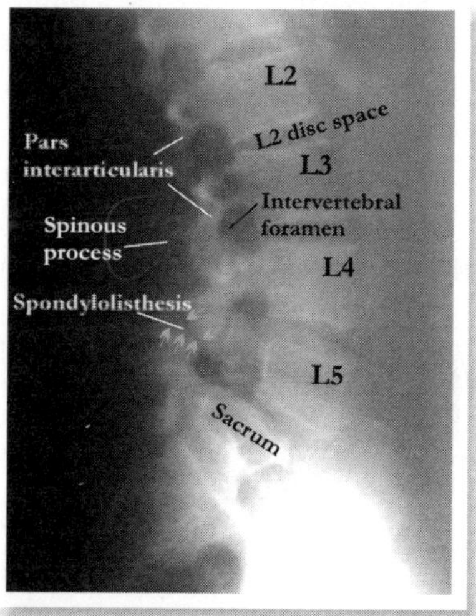

X-ray lumbosacral spine shows that the fifth lumbar vertebra has slipped froward in relation to the first piece of sacrum

condition is called spondylolisthesis. The doctor measures the displacement of the vertebra on a standing side (lateral) view X-ray of the spine. This way the extent of forward slippage is verified. If the vertebra is pressing on the nerves, a CT scan or MRI may be needed to further assess the abnormality, and see the actual extent of pressure on the spinal nerve roots.

Treatment

Treating spondylolysis

The initial treatment for spondylolysis is generally conservative. The individual should take a break from all vigorous activities until the symptoms go away, as they often do. Non-steroidal anti-inflammatory medications (NSAIDs) such as Ibuprofen may help reduce back pain. Occasionally, the doctor may recommend a back brace and physical therapy. In most cases, activities can be resumed gradually and there are few complications. Stretching and strengthening exercises for the back can help prevent future recurrences of pain.

However, surgery may be needed if the back pain does not respond to conservative treatment and begins to interfere with activities of daily life. In that case, a spinal fusion surgery is performed to plug the defect. Sometimes, an internal brace of screws and rods is used to hold together the fused vertebrae so that the fusion may become strong.

Treating spondylolisthesis

The decision about the type of treatment is made on the basis of the severity of the slip and the symptoms. If you have a spondylolisthesis, which is stable and non-progressive, you may do well without any treatment. Just so, it may be best to stay under a doctor's supervision, so that if the defect begins to widen, then proper treatment can be instituted in quick time.

If you have been diagnosed with spondylolisthesis, you should avoid activities that might cause more stress to the lumbar spine, such as sports activities like gymnastics, football, competitive swimming, and diving. Restrictions also apply on heavy lifting, excessive bending, twisting or stooping. You should discuss with a rehabilitation medicine physician about the necessary safeguards. You should also take advice about daily activities, which can be significant to your long-term physical and emotional well-being. Thus, you may find out that you can participate in swimming, walking in water, and regular walking, in addition to your back-strengthening physical therapy programme.

If you feel pain, your doctor may suggest non-steroidal anti-inflammatory pills like Ibuprofen and muscle relaxants.

You may also be asked to wear a corset or brace to provide additional support to the spine. This support may decrease muscle spasm and pain. Normally a corset is worn when you are up and about, but is often not necessary when you are lying in bed.

If you start wearing a corset, watch out for skin irritation (some redness is expected under the brace). If any sores on the skin are noted, remove your brace and contact your physician immediately for further skin-care instructions. The brace will be uncomfortable at first. It will take several days for you to begin to like your brace and the support that it gives your spine. Your brace should be worn under your clothing. Wearing your brace over clothing will cause increased pressure where waistbands, buckles, snaps and buttons can cause skin irritation and sores. You will need to wear a cotton undershirt that is snug-fitting under your brace to absorb moisture and prevent skin chaffing.

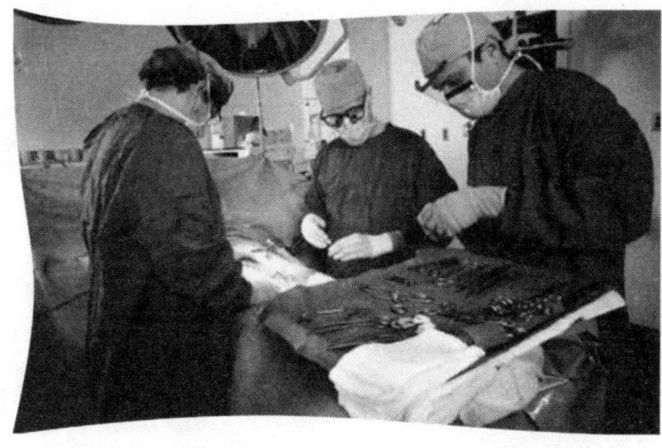

You may need to change the T-shirt a couple of times each day to remain comfortable. As soon as your back becomes stronger, your physician may restrict the use of the brace.

You may be advised surgery if your condition does not improve with these non-surgical measures. If the slippage is considerable at the time of the diagnosis, surgery may be suggested as the first course of treatment.

The goals of surgery are to remove pressure on spinal nerve roots, and to provide stability to the lumbar spine. In most cases of spondylolisthesis, lumbar decompression would need to be accompanied by uniting one spinal vertebra to the next (i.e. spinal fusion) with spinal implants that are often used to help aid the healing process.

15
Painful Small of the Back
The Sacro-iliac Joint Syndrome

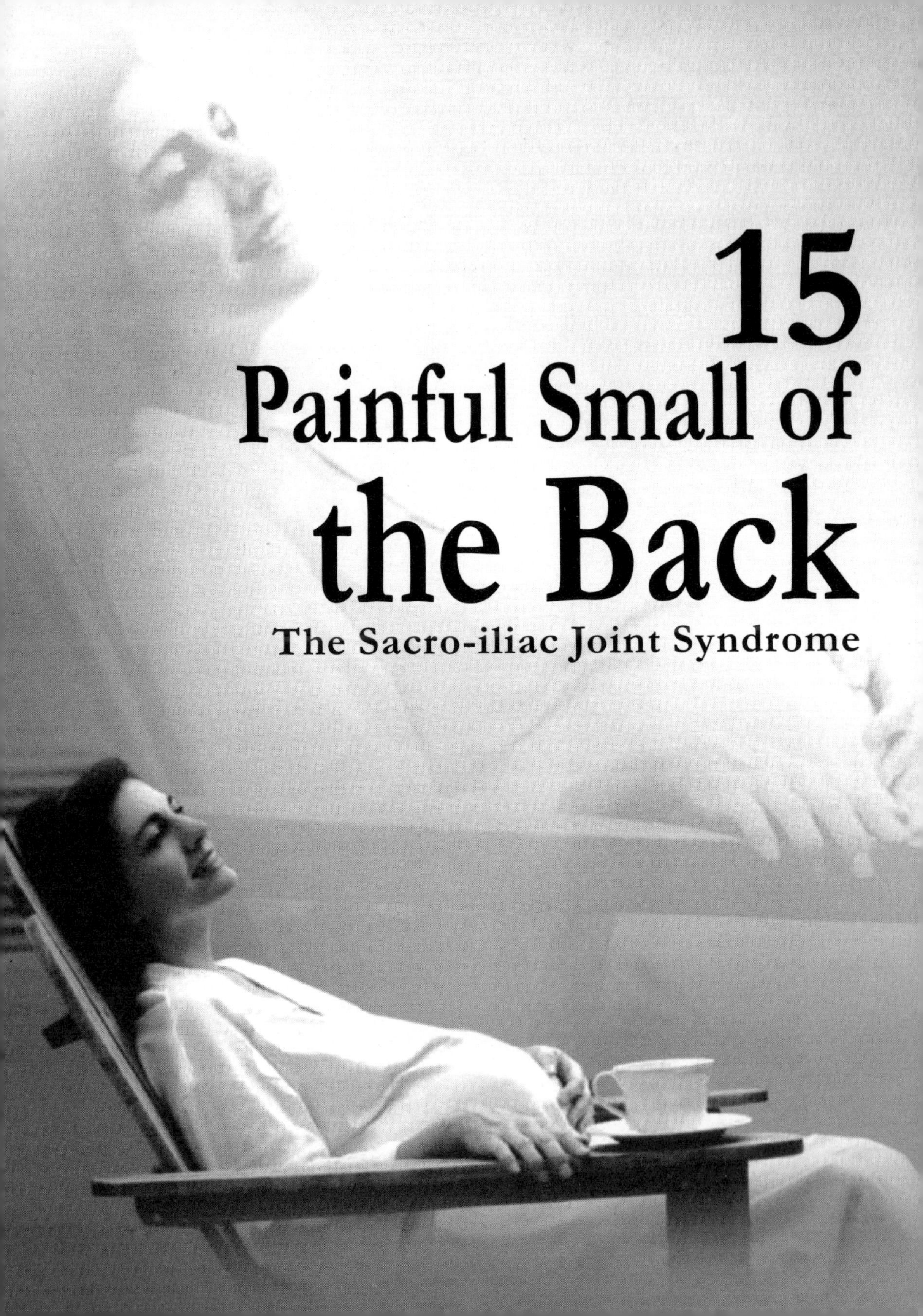

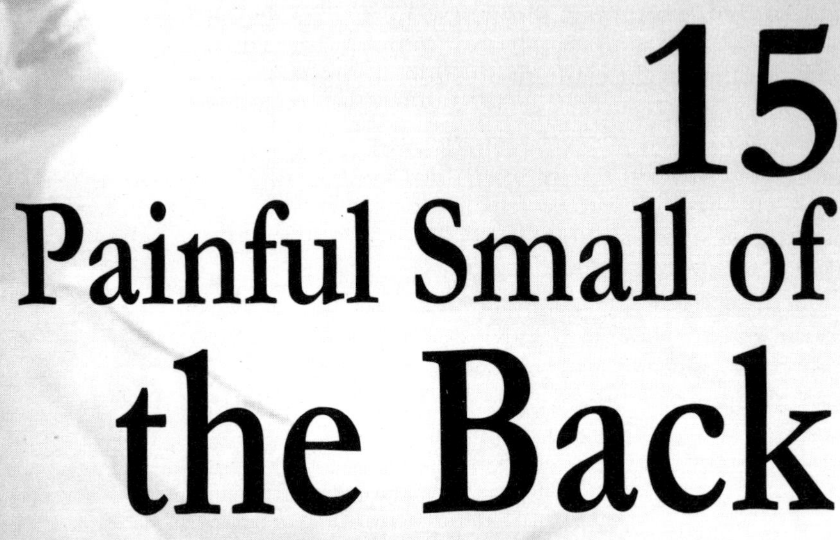

If you have pain in the small of the back, a little to the right or left of the mid line, just where the back hollows out above the buttocks, you could be afflicted with what doctors call the sacro-iliac joint syndrome.

A variety of conditions could be guilty, and if the problem has plagued you for some time now, it may be best to see a doctor. The pain could simply be due to sore muscles and tendons, strained overburdened sacro-iliac area due to flabby abdominal muscles and tight hamstrings, or more sinisterly, a slipped disc, a pinched nerve, a sore and swollen joint ridden with ankylosing spondylitis, rheumatoid arthritis or tuberculosis. If you are a young woman nurturing a pregnancy or a mother who has just given birth, think of it as just a mark of your motherly duties.

If you have a painful small of the back, digging the subject a bit deeper may have its rewards.

Fibrofascitis

If you have pain and stiffness in the small of the back, and a tender lump in the hollow above the buttocks, it's possible that your trouble may be related to a condition called fibrofascitis. This is a peculiar inflammation of the muscle and tendon sheaths over the sacro-iliac region. The capsule of the sacro-iliac joint may also be thickened and inflamed.

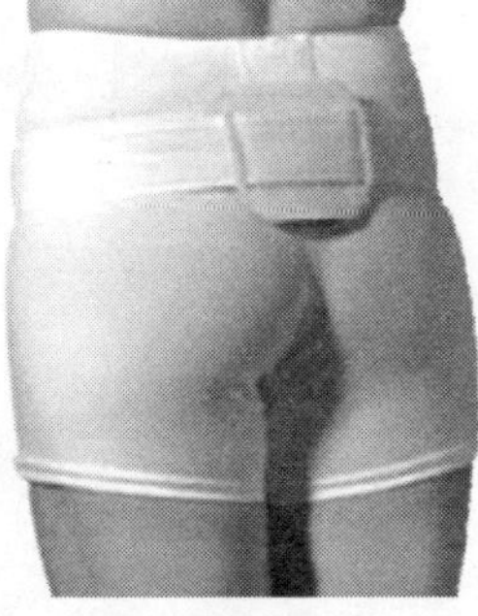

The diagnosis is largely clinical and based on the patient's physical examination. Even in normal people, small fibro-fatty lumps are sometimes visible and can be felt in the hollow above the buttocks on each side. But when a person has fibrofascitis, the lumps become more prominent and tender due to the inflammatory swelling in the region.

Sacro-iliac strain

In many people, the pain and stiffness relates to a chronic sacro-iliac strain, a condition caused by weak and poorly maintained abdominal muscles and tight hamstrings. The disorder is particularly common in people who lead a sedentary deskbound life, pay little attention to exercise and fitness and suffer from excess weight. This burdens the sacro-iliac region and places it under too much strain.

The condition can be diagnosed on the basis of the clinical history of the patient. X-rays and other tests do not demonstrate any abnormality.

Referred pain

In some people, the pain in the sacro-iliac region may be due to a far removed pathology and be a result of irritation of the nerve fibres that supply the area. The culprits could be many: a slipped disc between the fifth lumbar vertebra and first piece of sacrum or/and fourth and fifth lumbar vertebrae, wear-and-tear arthritis of the facet joints of the lower lumbar vertebrae, pinched spinal nerve roots in the spinal canal or neural foramina, or stretching of other pain-sensitive structures in the spine, such as the posterior longitudinal ligament, or ligamentum flavum.

In these situations, even though the pain has no direct pathological relationship to the sacro-iliac area, your doctor must read the situation correctly before a remedy can be found.

The sickly sacro-iliac joints

The sacro-iliac joints, located on each side of the midline, are large flat joints in the small of the back. They are formed between the wings of the pelvis and the right and left margins of the sacrum. The sacrum is a triangular block of bone built by five vertebral pieces glued together. It sits at the base of the spine, and is the weight-carrying foundation of the spinal column.

Unlike most other joints in the body, the sacro-iliac joints do not allow much movement between its member bones. Rather, they are rock solid joints, which

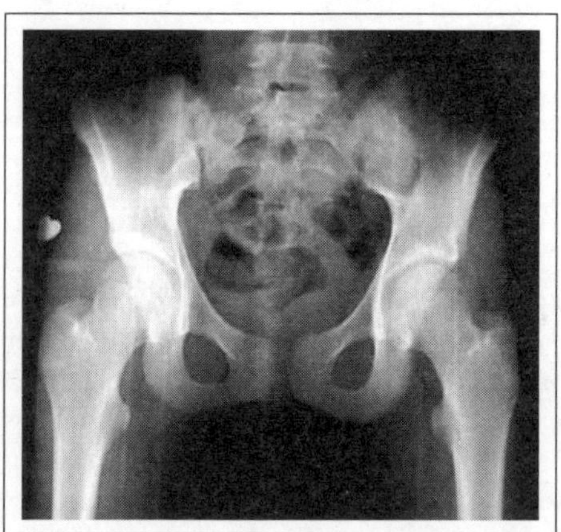

carry the body's total weight when it is in the upright stance.

The sacro-iliac joints can take considerable punishment without suffering any major wear-and-tear changes. However, they are often the seat of severe inflammation in a condition called ankylosing spondylitis, and may be affected by rheumatoid disease and also tuberculosis. These conditions are often picked on X-rays of the sacro-iliac joints, which can be done through different angles. They must be treated vigorously for the situation to improve.

Sacro-iliac joints and pregnancy

Women are particularly vulnerable to develop strain in the sacro-iliac joints. This happens during pregnancy, when the pelvic muscles and ligaments relax to meet the needs of the growing baby. When the mother delivers the baby, the pelvic joints, muscles and ligaments take a considerable stretching.

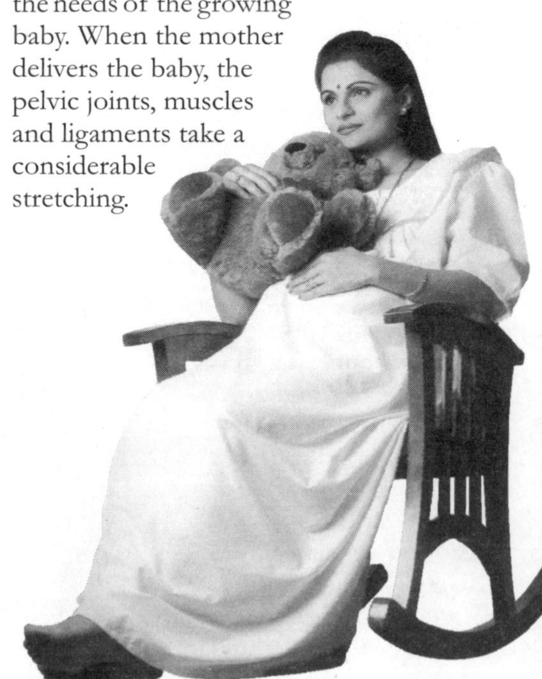

Both the situations can lead to mechanical pain in the sacro-iliac joints, but you can overcome the difficulty by being careful about your posture during pregnancy and being regular about pre-natal exercises during pregnancy and the back-fitness drill after your baby is born.

Treatment

The treatment of sacro-iliac joint syndrome is much like the treatment of backache, but if the condition relates to arthritic inflammation or tubercular infection of the sacro-iliac joint, more specific measures are called for. These treatments are dealt with elsewhere in this section where the focus is on those primary conditions.

In simpler situations, based on the acuteness and severity of the symptoms, the treatment entails resting in bed, a course of non-steroidal anti-inflammatory pills (NSAIDs), heat treatment, and use of pain-relieving gels and ointments to mitigate the pain. Those patients who are faced with severe muscle spasms may benefit by applying adhesive Belladonna tape and Capsicum ointment paste over the tender area. If the condition is severe and simple pain-relief treatments do not give relief, your doctor may decide to push a shot of locally acting Corticosteroids into the area.

Once the pain settles down, you must start with an active fitness programme. The key to betterment lies in strengthening the muscles of the abdomen, back and pelvis, and stretching out the hamstrings. Vitamin E may also be of some use. A woman just out of pregnancy and childbirth must also work on improving her fitness. She must tone up her lax ligaments and muscles before she can find relief. A sacro-iliac belt to support the lax ligaments and bind the flat pelvic bones together may provide extra relief.

For those who have arthritis of the sacro-iliac joint, and these simple measures do not ease the situation, a surgical fusion of the joint (arthrodesis) may be the way out. During surgery, the cartilage lining of the joint is removed, bone chips are filled into the defect, bone fragments are screwed together, and the healing is allowed to take place. The healing takes up to three months to complete, but vigorous outdoor activities must be avoided for a further period of three months.

16
Brittle Bones and Bad Backs
Osteoporosis

While you may think of bones as lifeless and rigid, they are actually a living tissue, which is being continuously broken down and rebuilt. When you are young, the rebuilding process takes precedence and the bones stay in the pink of health. But once a person grows older, the order gets reversed. Bone breakdown overtakes bone replacement, and the bones become thinner and lighter.

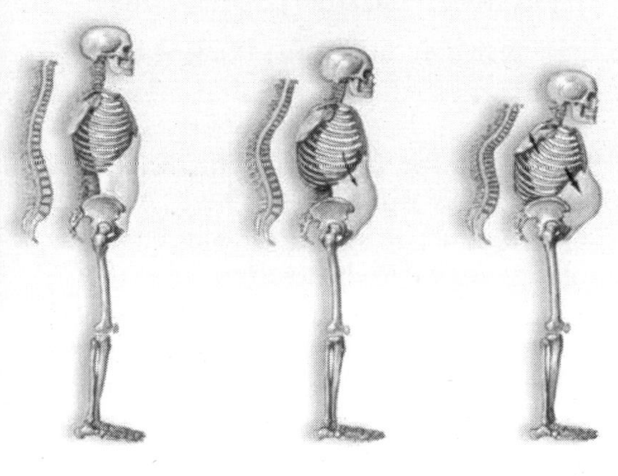

By the age of seventy-five, most people's skeletons are 40-50 per cent lighter than they were at the age of forty. This loss of bone tissue is known as osteoporosis. It results in bones that are brittle and liable to break.

Osteoporosis affects all the bones of the body. But because the backbone carries the body's weight, it is most vulnerable. Once the vertebrae become thin, they are easily crushed. This is a frequent cause of back pain and gradual loss of height in old people. The mid-back vertebrae often suffer the most, but in time, the entire spine is affected.

A share of the natural ageing process, osteoporosis affects all elderly people, but women suffer more severely than men, and at a comparatively younger age. On an average, one in two women, and one out of seven men, aged 50 or more, suffer from osteoporosis.

Factors that affect bone strength

A number of factors are vital to the rebuilding of bones in the body. Sex hormones are one. For this reason, when sex hormone production declines with age, osteoporosis sets in. In women, production of oestrogen drops rapidly when they attain menopause. This is when women begin to develop osteoporosis. Men are luckier in that they do not face andropause, but they also suffer a fall in the testosterone hormone with age.

Exercise is also a key factor. It is essential to maintain bone health. People who do little physical activity and those who are confined to bed because of a crippling illness suffer rapid bone loss. While those who lead an active life, suffer less.

Adequate supply of calcium and Vitamin D are also crucial to maintenance of bone strength. Low calcium diet, the social custom of staying fully covered head down in women, and the dark complexioned skin which is not conducive to the absorption of ultra-violet rays needed for the natural formation of Vitamin D, are factors that can deplete the stores of calcium and Vitamin D in the body.

Smoking, alcohol, too much caffeine and carbonic acid also tend to weaken the bones. If you go on a diet, it can also impact the bones adversely. Bone strength can also suffer because of other bodily diseases. People with chronic kidney failure, overactive thyroid gland, excessive parathyroid hormone, chronic infirmity, cancer or multiple myeloma are liable to develop brittle bones. Individuals on long-term oral Corticosteroids, such as patients of bronchial asthma, ulcerative colitis, rheumatoid arthritis, and autoimmune disorders also find it hard to escape the thinning of bones. Likewise, people on anti-epilepsy medications, anticoagulant (blood-thinning) therapy or chemotherapy also are prone to develop frail bones.

Prevention

You don't have to wait till you're 40 or above to begin active prevention against osteoporosis. The earlier you begin the better it is. The measures pay off best if started early in life. Teenagers and young adults should eat a balanced diet rich in calcium and Vitamin D and maintain this habit throughout life. Calcium is essential for bone strength, and Vitamin D aids calcium absorption in the body. Extra calcium is needed during pregnancy, while breast-feeding, and during and after menopause. Foods that contain good amounts of calcium include all dairy products, like milk, yoghurt, cheese and butter; some fresh fruits like oranges, custard apples and papaya; legumes, particularly lentils, beans and soya; some nuts such as almonds and walnuts; and some non-vegetarian foods like eggs, fish, chicken, and sea food. If your diet does not carry sufficient calcium, you should take calcium supplements. Vitamin D is also produced in the skin in response to sunlight. People exposed to little sunlight need Vitamin D supplements.

Walking and other weight-bearing exercise, such as running, dancing, aerobics or racquet sports are the best recipes to prevent osteoporosis. Yogic *asanas* also work well. There is good evidence that those who remain active into old age are less likely to suffer.

You must also limit alcohol intake and not smoke. Also, restrict tea, coffee, and cola drinks.

Symptoms

For many people, the first sign of osteoporosis is a sudden, severe back pain due to a compression fracture of the body of a vertebra. The fracture may follow a minor stress such as a bout of coughing, sneezing, or an unexpected jerk on a speed-breaker while in a car. If the osteoporosis is severe, a fracture may happen without warning or reason.

In time, osteoporosis often leads to a rounding of the back and gradual loss of height. These physical changes, which occur with age, arise due to the thinning of vertebrae and a loss in their height. Many people also suffer a wrist or hip fracture as a result of a minor fall.

Diagnosis

Diagnosis of osteoporosis is made on the basis of one's medical history, clinical examination and specialized tests. Your doctor may ask you to undergo bone densitometry, X-rays and blood work to confirm the diagnosis, and to look for other disorders that may cause osteoporosis.

The test of bone densitometry has become quite popular with increasing awareness of osteoporosis. The test can be done in two ways: while one way is to use ultrasound and measure bone density at the heel, the other is to use low-dose X-rays and measure the density of bones at different places. Both techniques are painless. Though the ultrasound test is relatively less reliable, but it has the advantage over X-ray densitometry as it is completely radiation-free. While ultrasound densitometry takes less than five minutes, X-ray densitometry takes about 10-20 minutes. Once the data is collected, a computer calculates the average density of the bone and compares it with the normal range for the person's age and sex.

Until bone densitometry came to the fore, the diagnosis was largely made on the basis of X-rays of the spine. But X-rays can only pick advanced osteoporosis; they may detect the change only when nearly 70 per cent of the calcium from the bone is lost.

Treatment

If you have back pain due to a fracture, your doctor may recommend rest in bed, use of pain-killers and a heating pad. You may also be asked to wear a lumbar brace for a few weeks. If the tests reveal any underlying disorder, your doctor will prescribe the appropriate treatment. For example, you may be prescribed pills to treat an overactive thyroid gland.

To slow the progression of osteoporosis, you must take active preventive measures described above. Your doctor may also prescribe medicines that check bone loss. These include such medicines as the selective estrogen receptor modulators like Raloxiphene; bisphosphonates like Sodium Alendronate, Pamidronate and Etidronate; and Calcitonin. There is evidence that bisphosphonates may also reduce the risk of fractures.

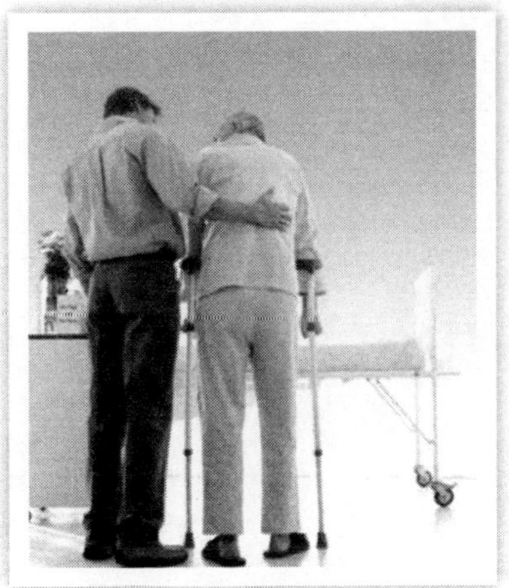

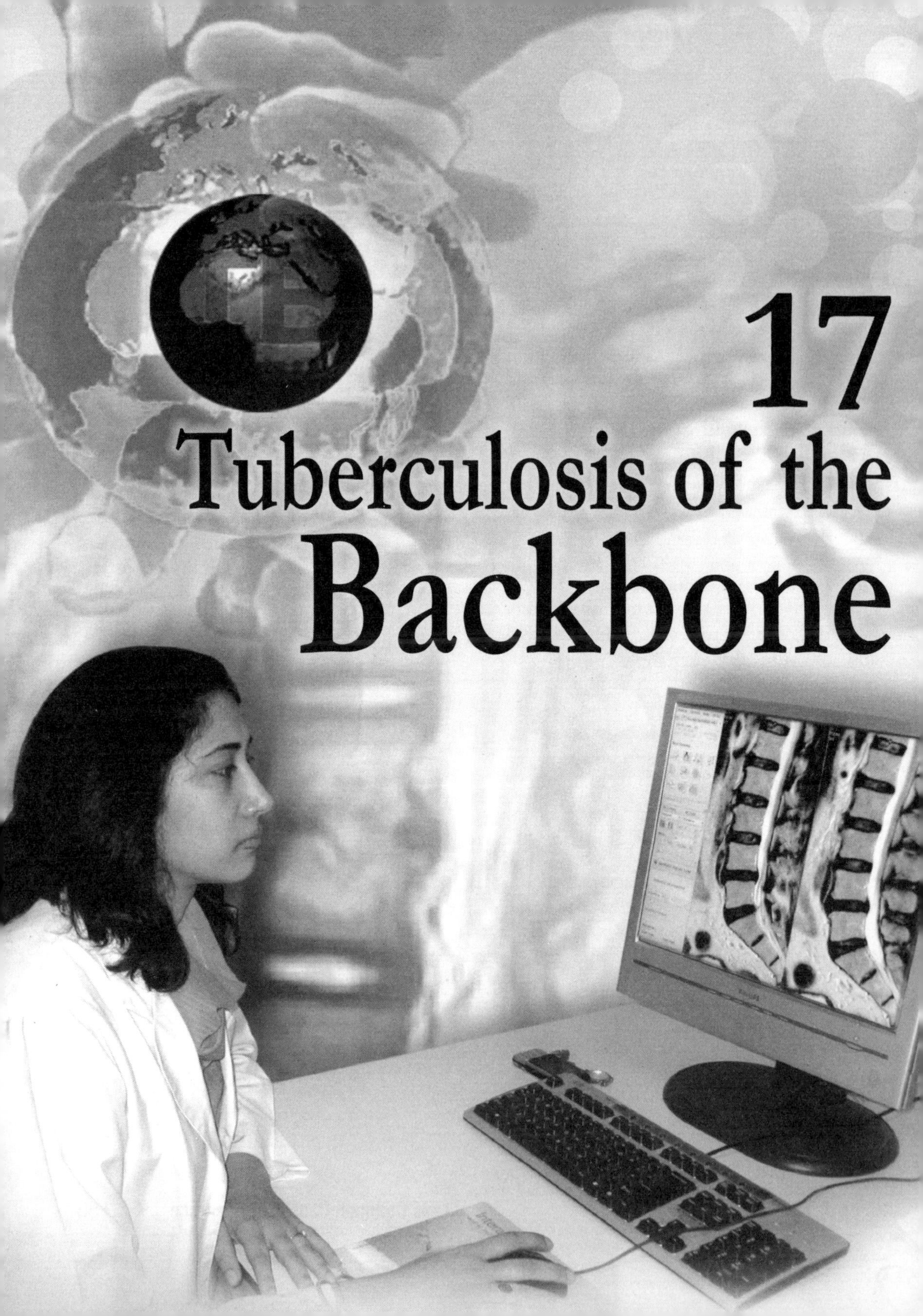

17 Tuberculosis of the Backbone

Tuberculosis, once called *raja rog*, *rajyakshma*, consumption and white plague, is an ancient disease that may have always riddled the human race. The oldest evidence of the disease comes from the Egyptian mummies, which date back to around 2,000 BC. Records of tuberculosis are found in the ancient Hindu, Chinese, Babylonian and Egyptian texts. *Atharva Veda*, one of the four oldest scriptures of Hinduism, presents a most vivid portrayal of its symptoms and terms it a most difficult disease to treat.

The first major breakthrough against tuberculosis was made on March 24, 1882 when Robert Koch, a German physician, announced to the Berlin Physiological Society that he had discovered the cause of the disease. He named the causative organism *Mycobacterium tuberculosis*. Three weeks later, on April 10, he published an article entitled 'The Aetiology of Tuberculosis'.

This was a big discovery. Still, the conquest of tuberculosis was relatively slow. It was not until the 1950s that the first effective line of anti-tubercular drugs, Streptomycin, Para Amino-Salicylate (PAS) and Isoniazid (INH) were discovered, and the disease became curable.

In the last 50 years, scientists have discovered several new anti-tubercular medicines, and this has cut short the duration of treatment, but tuberculosis continues to be rife all across the globe. Still, the 'captain of death', it causes more deaths than any other single infectious organism. Currently, 8 million new cases of active tuberculosis are diagnosed annually, resulting in one death every 10 seconds. A third of the global population is latently infected with the organism and at risk of developing active disease.

Tuberculosis can strike any part of the body, but lungs are most commonly stricken. Next, in order, are the intestines. But bone and joint tuberculosis is also fairly common, and spine is the favoured site.

Spinal tuberculosis

Tuberculosis can strike any vertebra, but those that lie at the back of the chest, called the thoracic vertebrae, are most commonly affected. Often, the disease attacks two or more adjoining vertebrae at the same time, and causes a widespread destruction of the bone and the intervening disc.

Symptoms

Depending on the severity of illness, a number of symptoms can appear. The commonest is a varying degree of pain in the back. The pain classically awakens the sufferer at night, causing what's known as 'night cries'.

If the vertebrae give way, the dorsal spine collapses forward and develops an acute forward bend, causing a hunchback. Since the spinal canal is fairly narrow in this part, this structural collapse and the accumulation of tubercular pus puts the spinal cord under pressure. The victim may develop a number of neurological symptoms and signs and suffer weakness of the legs that could worsen over a few days, leading to paralysis and inability to stand. Bladder and bowel control also may be lost.

The collection of pus at various sites may also produce adverse symptoms. Some

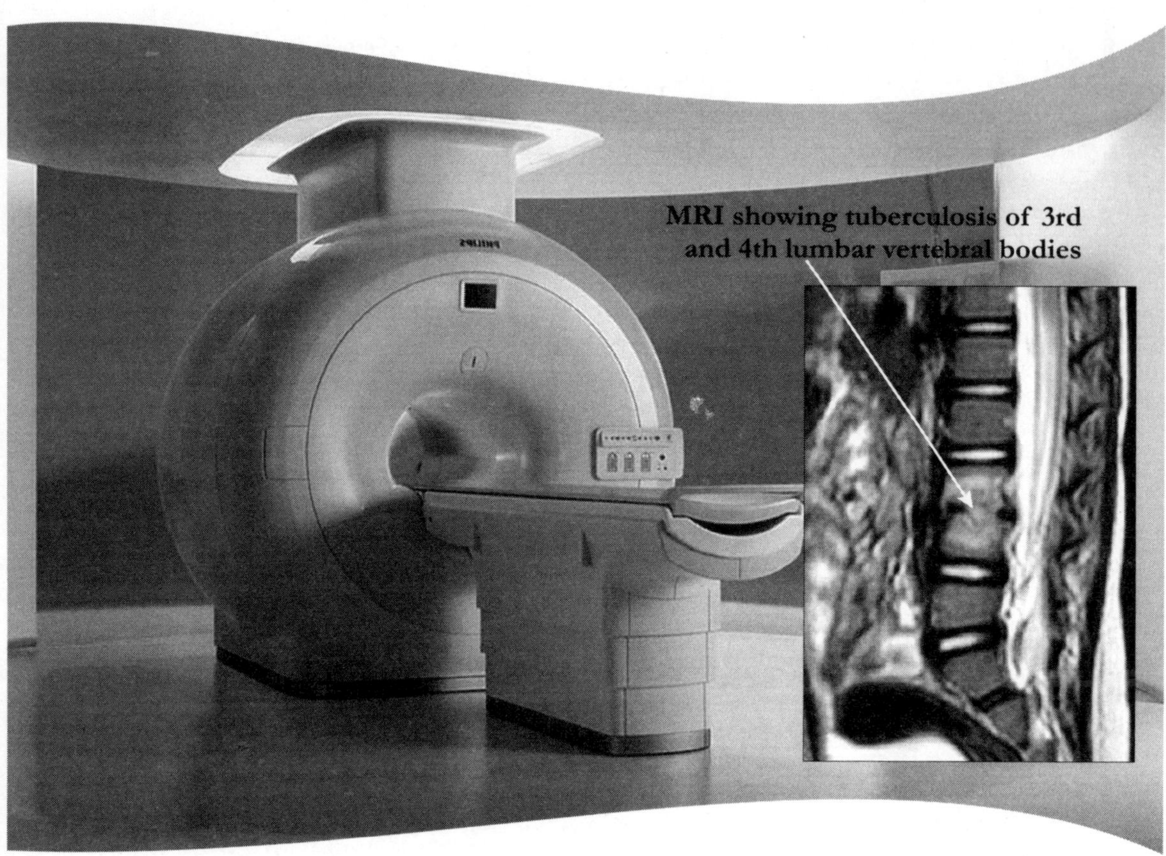

MRI showing tuberculosis of 3rd and 4th lumbar vertebral bodies

people develop a boggy swelling on one side of the spine, others a cold abscess in the groin, and a few people a collection along the ribs. The pus can also track into the skin.

A person with tuberculosis is likely to suffer from low-grade fever. The temperature typically rises each evening. He or she may also have sweating at night, cough, blood spitting, and suffer an acute loss of weight. None of the symptoms are peculiar to tuberculosis, but if they occur, they make the diagnosis of tuberculosis more likely. Continued ill health is a most constant symptom.

Diagnosis

If you have the classic symptoms, your doctor might think of tuberculosis and investigate for it. However, often the diagnosis is made on chance on an X-ray of the chest or dorso-lumbar spine. Blood work, including the cell counts and erythrocyte sedimentation rate (ESR), a polymerised chain reaction (PCR) test on blood, urine, human secretions or a pus aspirate, and a tuberculin skin test can offer useful corroborative evidence.

Treatment

Treatment of spinal tuberculosis needs a long-term commitment. The line of treatment varies with the severity and extent of disease. If there are no neurological signs, anti-tubercular drugs (including Isoniazid, Rifampicin, Ethambutol and Pyrazinamide), bed rest and a spinal support (spinal jacket, dorso-lumbar brace, Minerva brace, or cervical collar) shape the treatment.

The drug treatment in bone and joint tuberculosis has to be much more rigorous than in lung tuberculosis. Anti-tubercular medicines must be taken, without fail for a period of at least 18 months. While four medicines are given for the first few months, three are necessary for the rest of the period. You cannot afford to be careless with the medicines. If you neglect the treatment, you run a risk that the bacteria may develop resistance to the medications and the treatment could be a total failure.

Surgery may be necessary if there is widespread loss of bone and pus formation, and a danger to the spinal cord, which may suffer compression if surgical care is not exercised. The operation is done under either general or local anaesthesia, once you have begun the anti-tubercular medication. The key objective is to clear the pockets of pus and dying tissues completely, and restrict the damage. Delay in surgery can some-times lead to irreparable loss of function.

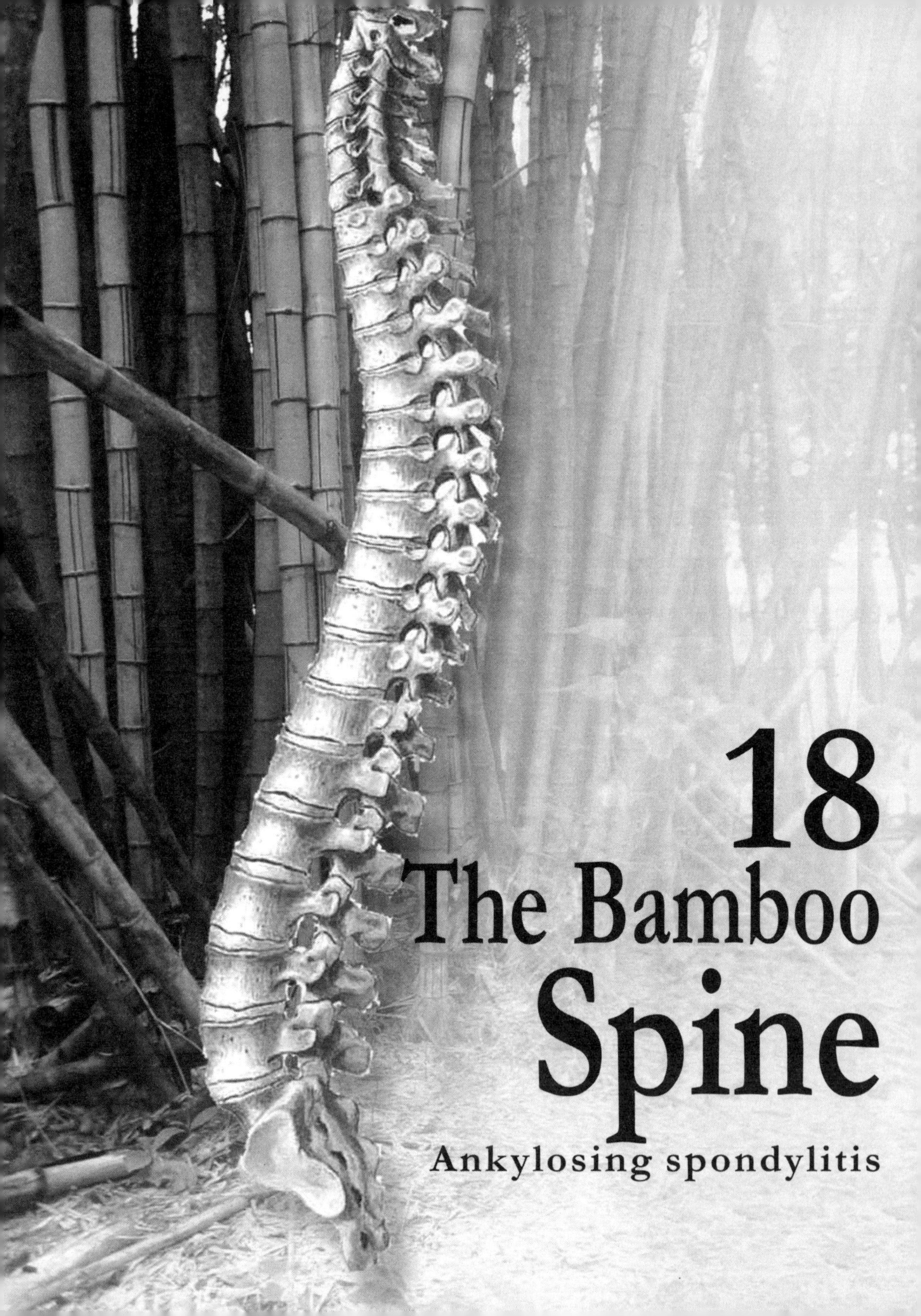

18 The Bamboo Spine

Ankylosing spondylitis

Ankylosing spondylitis is a persistent inflammatory disease of the spinal column and the pelvis that causes stiffening of the affected joints. While the spine takes the maximum damage, the sacro-iliac joints at the back of the pelvis and the hip joints are often affected. If the spine is severely diseased, new bone grows between the vertebrae, which eventually fuse together. This leads to such a severe hardening and stiffness of the spine that it begins to bear a striking resemblance to a bamboo stick.

The condition is much more common in men than in women. Usually, the disease begins in late adolescence or early adulthood, and in some families, it runs as a familial disease.

Causative factors

The cause of ankylosing spondylitis is unknown, but about 90 per cent affected people have a particular antigen (a substance that is capable of stimulating an immune response in the body) called HLA-B27 on the surface of most cells. This antigen is inherited. Most people with HLA-B27 do not develop the disease, but its presence predisposes them to develop the disease. A bacterial infection probably triggers the condition by fooling the immune system of the body to strike against its own tissues.

Symptoms

Classically, the disease appears in late adolescence or early adulthood and develops gradually over a period of months or years. The main symptoms include lower back pain and stiffness that may be worse in the morning and improves with activity.

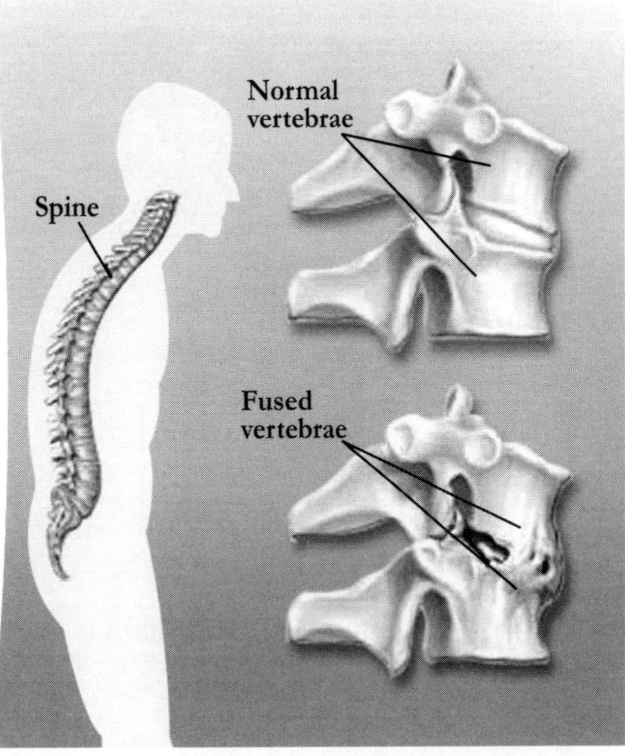

Classically, a male disease, ankylosing spondylitis causes fusion of the vertebral spine leading to stoop and crippling deformity of the back and the hips.

The sufferer may also have pain in other joints, such as the hips, knees, and shoulders, and pain and tenderness in the heels. At the same time, the person may feel tired and suffer mild fever and weight loss.

The disease can distort the spine and produce a stoop. In some people, due to the widespread inflammation in the body tissues other than the joints, such as eyes may also

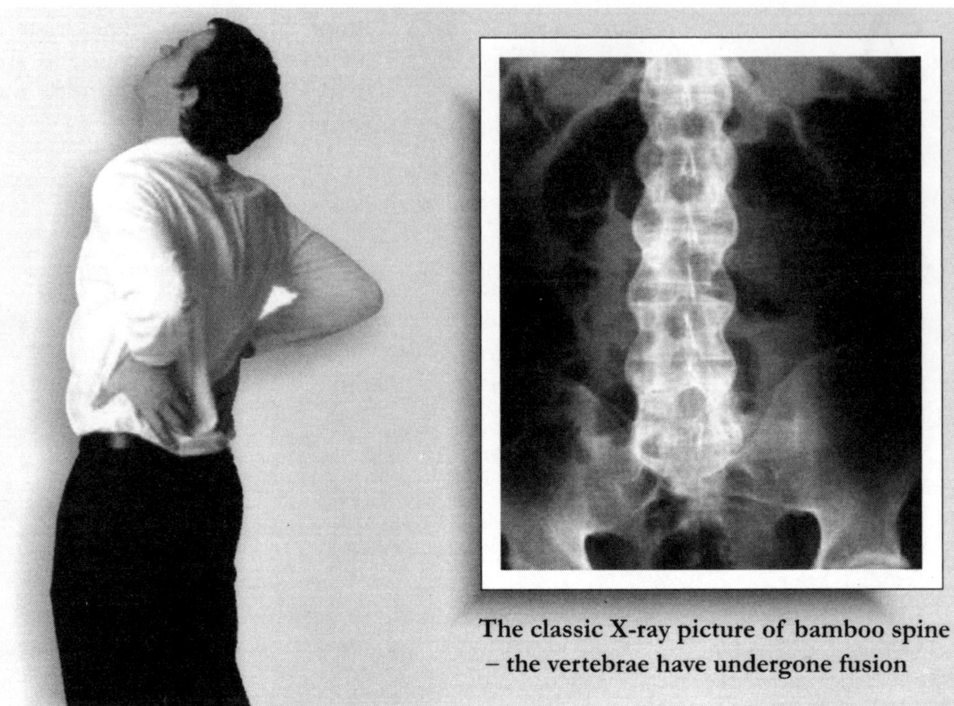

The classic X-ray picture of bamboo spine – the vertebrae have undergone fusion

be affected. Some people may also develop difficluty in breathing because they cannot expand the chest.

Diagnosis

The first suggestion of ankylosing spondylitis relates to the pattern of symptoms. Your doctor may suspect the diagnosis on that basis and ask for X-ray of the spine and sacro-iliac joints to look for evidence of fusion in these joints. You may also be asked to undergo blood tests including HLA-B27 antigen, ESR, blood counts and others that look for evidence of inflammation.

Treatment

Treatment of ankylosing spondylitis is aimed at relieving the symptoms and preventing the development of spinal deformity. You may be prescribed a non-steroidal anti-inflammatory drug (NSAID) like Indomethacin to control pain and inflammation. At the same time, you must also begin on an active exercise programme under the care of a physiatrist and a physiotherapist. Breathing exercises, and daily exercises to help improve your posture, strengthen the back muscles and prevent deformities of the spine must make an essential part of your routine.

To relieve pain, other pain-relief measures such as hot fomentation with wet packs, hot baths, sauna and massage may also be usefully employed. Some doctors also prefer to treat with intravenous Corticosteroids, followed by oral steroids tapered over a period of weeks or months, to good relief.

You may also benefit from regular physical activity, such as swimming, which may help to relieve pain and stiffness.

Surgery may also be useful if a joint, such as a hip is affected. A total hip replacement can restore good function to the joint and relieve deformity and disability.

Although ankylosing spondylitis is not curable, most people can lead a fairly decent life unless the disease is severe. Early treatment and regular exercise are the best options to relieve the pain and stiffness of the back and prevent deformity of the spine.

19
The Muscular Back Pain
Fibromyalgia

Quite a few adult people, particularly women, suffer from body pain, stiffness and tiredness associated with pervasive muscle tenderness. Still, when they are tested for any abnormality in the muscle tissue or the biochemistry or serology of the body, no fault can be made out. This unexplainable disorder particularly develops during periods of constant worry and strain, and for that reason, is thought to be a fall-out of stress. The condition is called fibromyalgia.

Symptoms

The muscle pain and tenderness of fibromyalgia develops slowly over weeks and is not limited only to the back. Usually, it follows a distinct pattern around the body. The sufferer complains of muscle pain in the upper back, head, thighs, abdomen and hips and, if anybody palpates or applies pressure on her or his muscles, they feel tender. Such tenderness is especially felt at the upper end of the neck and near the shoulder blades. She may also suffer tingling and numbness in the hands and feet.

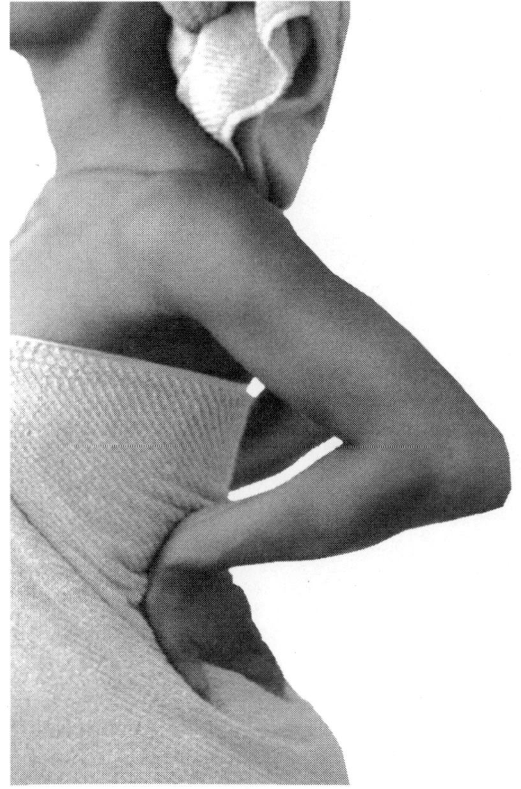

Many people suffering from fibromyalgia are also plagued by several other ailments. They may suffer from headaches, anxiety, tiredness, depression and disturbed sleep patterns. Some people also have irregular bowel movements. These symptoms represent the adrenaline-sparked high inner stress, which affects both the mind and the body of the person.

Diagnosis

The diagnosis of fibromyalgia is often based on the symptoms and a physical examination, but your doctor may arrange for blood tests to rule out other conditions, such as connective tissue disorders. These tests draw a blank, but rule out such major conditions as rheumatoid arthritis and lupus, which need a different line of treatment.

The tender areas (trigger points)

The pressure areas called trigger points are quite classical. They are generally symmetrical, and are most commonly sited in the following places in the body:

- A point in the back portion of the head

- A point midway between the back of the head and the middle of the back
- A point above the shoulder blade
- A point where the second rib joins the breastbone
- A point two inches below the outer back portion of the elbow
- A point in the upper outer quarter of the buttock
- A point on the hipbone on which a person sits
- A point on the fat pad above the inner joint line of the knee

If these points feel tender, you may think that you are suffering from fibromyalgia.

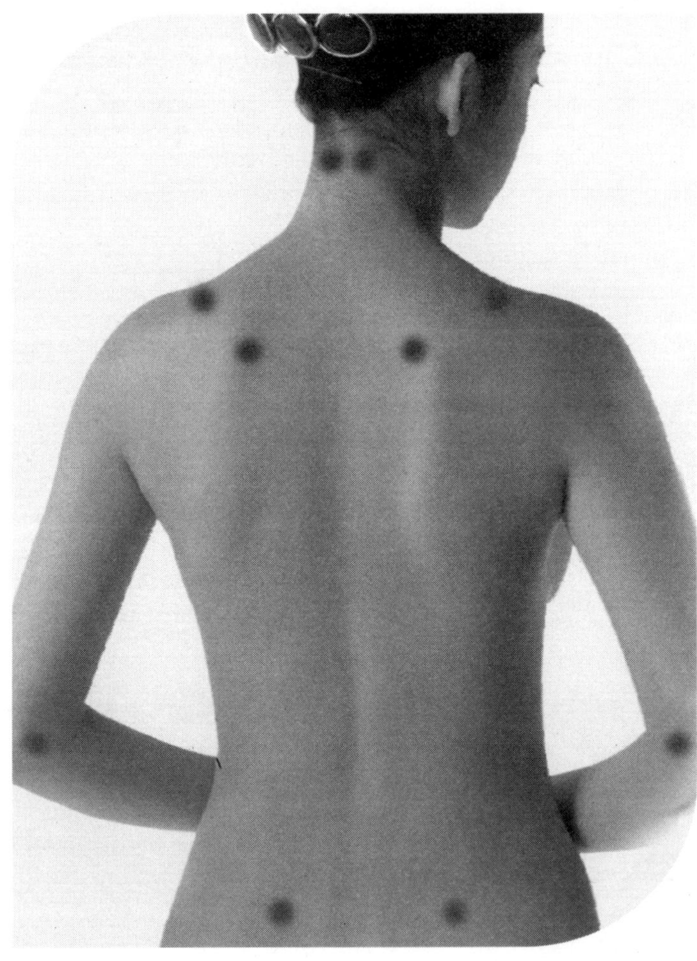

Treatment

If you have been recently diagnosed with fibromyalgia, the first fundamental step you must take is to calm down and get rid of the unhealthy stress. Stop worrying and start living. In addition, if you're having any other medical problem such as overweight, high blood pressure, migraine, hypothyroidism or menstrual irregularity, take proper treatment and control the problem.

The pain of fibromyalgia may be relieved by deep tissue massage and locally applied moist heat, ultrasound treatment, short-wave diathermy, interferential therapy, transcutaneous nerve stimulation or an injection with a local anaesthetic. Your doctor may also prescribe a low dosage of Amitriptyline, an antidepressant pill, to relieve pain. The medicine must be taken for at least two or three weeks before you would feel any improvement.

You must also incorporate a regular exercise programme in your daily plan. Take a brisk walk, perform stretching exercises, strengthen your muscles, and you could well be on the road to a full recovery.

20
Backaches of a
Different Kind

Back pain may not always reflect a spinal disorder. Conditions in a different place in the body may also sometimes present with backache. In these situations, the back pain is often accompanied by other symptoms that are more representative of the condition.

Gynaecological disorders

Women often complain of low back pain in a number of gynaecological disorders. Menstrual cramps are a known cause of dull generalized low back pain; infections of the reproductive tract can cause low backache; while a prolapsed womb can be associated with a dull, dragging pain in the lower back.

Kidney conditions

Both men and women can suffer back pain in a number of assorted conditions. A large number of back pain victims actually have a kidney problem. For instance, a constant dull low back pain, often limited to one or both loins, accompanied by fever and discoloured urine generally indicate a kidney infection. A stone in the kidney can cause intermittent sharp pain in the lower back, which may be accompanied by nausea and vomiting.

Pancreas, bowel and the heart

Inflammation in the pancreas, a condition called pancreatitis, that's common in people who binge or suffer from gallstones, can cause a severe pain in the pit of the stomach and mid-back. Duodenal and stomach ulcers can also cause burning pain in the mid-back. Rarely, even a bad heart affected with coronary heart disease can also present with back pain.

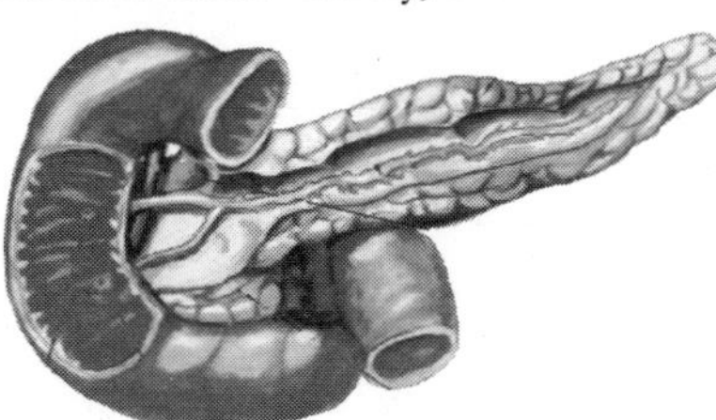

Cancers

Spread of cancer to the bones in the spine, leukaemia, lymphoma and multiple myeloma can also produce backache due to the spread of the disease into the vertebrae.

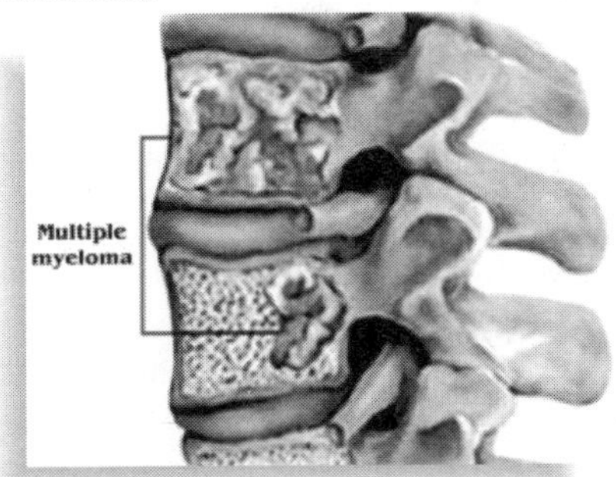

What to do?

In most situations, your doctor is able to pick the diagnosis. He or she may ask you to undergo an X-ray, an ultrasound or another test to confirm his or her suspicion. The bottom line is – never neglect pain. Think of pain as a danger bell the body rings to tell you that something is wrong. You must act well on time and take the help of your doctor. He or she can help find the cause and treat the condition in the best possible way.

Glossary

Acute

Of recent origin, occurring suddenly and painfully; short duration (compare chronic).

Analgesic

A pain-relieving substance or drug.

Ankylosing spondylitis

A form of arthritis in which the joints of the spine gradually stiffen and can become rigid.

Avulsion

A fracture in which the tip of a bony process, one of the protrusions at the rear of the vertebrae, is cracked or pulled off.

Brachialgia

Pain in the arm and/or hand that may be caused by compression of a nerve. It may be accompanied by numbness or pins and needles and muscle weakness.

Cartilage

The tough and slippery covering at the end of bones where they meet to form joints.

Cauda equina

The sheaf of nerves that fan out from the bottom of the spinal cord.

Cervical spine

The part of the spine that forms the neck.

Chronic

Of long duration.

Compression

Pressure on a nerve or the spinal cord, perhaps by a prolapsed disc.

Crush fracture

The collapse of a vertebra.

Disc (intervertebral disc)

A fibrous shock-absorbing pad that sits between the individual vertebrae.

Dural sleeves

The sheaths encasing and protecting the nerve roots as they branch off from the spinal cord.

Dural tube

The sheath of the spinal cord, which consists of three membranes, the meninges, one inside the other.

Epidural

An injection of pain-killing drugs into the spinal canal in the lower back.

Facet joint

One of the chain of small joints that link the bony processes at the rear of the vertebrae to each other.

Ligament

A band of tough, fibrous tissue that supports bones at a joint and controls the way in which they can move.

Lumbago

Pain in the lower back.

Lumbar

Relating to the lower part of the spine, from the waist to the hips.

Micro-fracture

A tiny fracture in the flat, weight-bearing surface of a vertebra where it joins the disc or in one of the transverse processes, the bony protrusions at the back of the vertebrae.

Osteophytes

Bony, spur-like growths on or around the vertebrae. Osteophytes are a feature of osteoarthritis.

Osteoporosis

A condition in which bones become thin and brittle, normally associated with ageing.

Process, bony or transverse

One of three protrusions at the rear of each vertebra, which joins the vertebrae together, at the facet joints.

Prolapsed disc

The rupture of a disc's outer casing and the leakage of a part of its nucleus.

Rehabilitation medicine

Medical speciality concerned with the treatment of chronic disabilities and with the restoration of normal functioning to the disabled through physical modes of treatment, such as exercise. This specialized medical service is generally aimed at rehabilitating persons disabled by pain or ailments affecting the motor functions of the body. Physical medicine is one means employed to assist these patients to return to a comfortable and productive life, often despite the persistence of a medical problem. Physical medicine is closely associated with orthopaedic surgery. Physicians who specialize in physical medicine are called physiatrists.

The objectives of physical medicine are relief of pain, improvement or maintenance of function, strength and mobility, and retraining the patient to carry out his essential activities.

Sacralization

A condition in which the lowest lumbar vertebra is fused to the sacrum and becomes a fixed part of the pelvis.

Sacro-iliac joints

The two joints that join the bottom of the spine to the pelvis. Frequently, the site of strain in young people and pregnant women.

Sacrum

The wedge-shaped bone sandwiched between the two hipbones (ilia), on which the spine rests.

Scheuermann's disease

A developmental disorder of the growing parts of the vertebral bodies, generally giving rise to an excessive rounding of the spine.

Schmorl's nodes

A bulging of disc material into the vertebral bodies, commonly multiple and occurring in more than a third of spines.

Sciatica

Pain of whatever cause radiating down the back of the leg along the distribution of the sciatic nerve. It may be accompanied by numbness or pins and needles. Sciatica can be caused by the compression of a sciatic nerve, perhaps by a prolapsed disc.

Scoliosis

A lateral or sideways curvature of the spine.

Senile kyphosis

An increased rounding of the spine brought about by a loss of thickness of the spinal discs and often aggravated by a weakening of bone texture and consequent wedging of the vertebrae.

Slipped disc

See prolapsed inter-vertebral disc.

Spina bifida

A congenital deformity in which the spinal canal fails to close fully. In severe cases this may allow the nerve tissues to protrude through the spine.

Spinal canal

The bony channel formed from the neural arch through which the spinal cord runs.

Spinal stenosis

A narrowing of the spinal canal, through which the spinal cord passes, perhaps by a prolapsed disc or by the growth of osteophytes.

Spinous processes

The bony knobs at the back of the vertebrae which provide attachment for muscles, ligaments and fascia.

Spondylolisthesis

A condition of the spine in which the vertebral arch breaks right through and the vertebra slips out of line. It is often a progression of spondylolysis.

Spondylolysis

A fracture in the vertebral arch; it is most common in the lower lumbar spine.

Spondylosis

A degenerative process associated with a loss of resilience and thickness of the spinal discs, osteoarthritis of the intervertebral joints and the formation of bony spurs around the rim of the vertebral bodies.

Synovial fluid

A fluid that lubricates the joints.

Tendon

A tough band of tissue connecting muscle to the bone.

Thoracic spine

The part of the spine from the neck to the waist.

Tomography

A computer-aided scanning technique for obtaining sectional pictures of the body, known as computerized tomography or CT.

Vertebra (plural vertebrae)

One of the individual bones of the spine.

Vertebral arch

A bony arch at the rear of each vertebra. The arches of all the vertebrae together form the spinal canal through which the spinal cord runs.

Whiplash injury

A strain or tear injury to the ligaments supporting the bones of the neck. It usually occurs when the head is thrown violently backward and forward as in a car crash.

Wry neck

Pain and restricted movement in the neck that may be the result of a facet joint or disc problem.

Backache: Common types, cause and treatment

Problem	Likely cause	Possible treatment
Pain and stiffness in the back	Strained back due to postural stress	1. *Initial:* apply a hot towel, use painkiller pills and analgesic ointment 2. *Long term:* correct posture; check if there's any environmental factor, e.g. poorly designed desk or chair causing undue stress on the back 3. Regular exercises to strengthen the muscles of the back, abdomen, neck and hamstrings
Pain and stiffness in lower/mid-back; may be accompanied by pain in buttocks/ hips/ thighs	Back strain/possibly prolapsed disc	1. Restrict painful activity 2. Apply a hot towel, use painkiller pills, and rub on an analgesic ointment 3. Regular exercises to strengthen the muscles of the back, abdomen, neck and hamstrings
Pain and stiffness in the neck	Neck strain/possibly disc problem	1. Restrict painful activity 2. Wrap a hot towel, use painkiller pills, and lightly apply an analgesic ointment 3. Regular exercises to strengthen the neck muscles
Pain in the neck with restriction of movements a few hours following an accident which led to jolting of the neck	Whiplash injury	1. Visit your doctor to rule out any serious injury 2. Rest, wrap a cold towel, use painkiller pills, and lightly apply an analgesic ointment 3. *Long term:* Regular neck exercises
Pain in the leg on bending forward	Sciatic nerve irritation	1. Specific exercises for the back muscles and hamstrings 2. Epidural steroid injection
Acute low back pain usually to one side, possibly after bending strain	Disc prolapse	1. *Initial:* wrap a hot towel, use painkiller pills and analgesic ointment 2. *Later:* physiotherapy and exercises, esp. spinal. abdominal and hamstring stretch 3. Epidural steroid injection/acupuncture
Pain in low back going down one leg, may be accompanied by a pins -and-needles sensation	Disc prolapse with compression of the nerve root	1. *Initial:* wrap a hot towel, use painkiller pills and analgesic ointment 2. *Later:* physiotherapy and exercises, esp. spinal, abdominal and hamstring stretch 3. Epidural steroid injection/acupuncture

Problem	Likely cause	Possible treatment
Pain in upper back radiating down one arm, possibly with pins and needles	Disc prolapse causing compression of nerve root	1. *Initial:* apply a hot towel, use painkiller pills and analgesic ointment 2. *Later:* physiotherapy and exercises, esp. neck exercises 3. Nerve block/acupuncture
Pain just above the buttock	Sacro-iliac strain or fibrofasciitis	1. *Initial:* apply a hot towel, use painkiller pills and analgesic ointment 2. *Later:* physiotherapy and exercises, esp. spinal, abdominal and hamstring stretch 3. Steroid injection in the painful region
Constant low back pain and stiffness over the sacro-iliac joint, worse at night, mostly affecting young males, lasting weeks to months	Ankylosing spondylitis	1. Anti-inflammatory analgesics and rest 2. Physiotherapy to maintain flexibility and mobility of the spine 3. If deformities occur, you may require surgery
Mid back pain, ill health, night sweats, loss of appetite, possibly weakness and paralysis of legs, bladder and bowel	Tuberculosis of the spine	1. Consult an orthopaedic specialist 2. Rest, and use a brace to support your back 3. Anti-tubercular medications 4. Sometimes surgery
Severe, constant back pain in the elderly	Osteoporotic fracture	1. Consult an orthopaedic surgeon and take the prescribed tests 2. Rest, use a brace to support your back and take painkillers 3. Calcium, Vitamin D, and other medication
Severe back pain with numbness or tingling in the legs	Spondylolisthesis	1. Consult an orthopaedic surgeon 2. Rest, use a brace to support your back and painkillers 3. Physiotherapy 4. Some may need surgery

Problem	Likely cause	Possible treatment
Pain, tingling or numbness in the leg; symptoms worsen on walking, less severe if you sit or bend forward	Spinal canal stenosis	1. Consult an orthopaedic surgeon 2. Rest, analgesics 3. Physiotherapy 4. Some may need surgery
Pain in back/legs, with weakness, numbness loss of bladder or bowel sensation/control	Compression of spinal cord/cauda equina or prolapsed disc	1. Seek urgent medical help. Consult an orthopaedic surgeon or neurosurgeon. 2. CT or MRI to confirm the type and level of lesion 3. Urgent surgery a definite possibility
Back pain, fever, tiredness	Epidural abscess	1. Seek urgent medical help. Consult an orthopaedic surgeon 2. Antibiotics
Back pain, generalized body ache, fever	Viral fever	1. Rest 2. Plenty of fluids 3. Fever and pain-relieving medicines
Back pain, stiff neck, fever	Meningitis	1. Seek urgent medical help. Consult a physician/paediatrician
Severe colicky pain, right upper abdomen, pain over right shoulder blade	Gall bladder inflammation/ stones	1. Consult a surgeon 2. Ultrasound of the abdomen to confirm the diagnosis 3. Surgery
Spasmodic pain in the loin, or colicky pain in the loin travelling to the testis/vulva, and nausea	Kidney or ureter stones	1. Consult a surgeon 2. Ultrasound/ X-ray abdomen to confirm the diagnosis 3. Treatment will depend on the size and location of the stone, the existing facilities, and the personal preference of surgeon and the patient
Severe pain in the pit of stomach, mid back penetrating pain, vomiting, sometimes also jaundice	Pancreatitis	1. Consult a surgeon 2. Ultrasound/ CT abdomen, specific blood tests to confirm the diagnosis 3. Hospitalization, rest and supportive treatment

Problem	Likely cause	Possible treatment
Burning or penetrating pain in mid-or low back many hours after partaking food	Duodenal ulcer	1. Consult a gastroenterologist 2. Upper GI endoscopy to confirm the diagnosis 3. Acid-blocking medication, antacids, bland diet
Low back pain in a young woman	Premenstrual or menstrual pain	1. Hot bath 2. Pain-relievers 3. Relaxation techniques/yoga
In a woman, back/ abdominal pain, vaginal discharge and or pain during coitus	Uterine/fallopian tubes infection	1. Consult a gynaecologist 2. Microscopic examination of vaginal smear 3. Antibiotics
In a woman, dragging pain in lower back	Prolapsed uterus	1. Consult a gynaecologist 2. Diagnosis by physical examination 3. Surgery

Acknowledgements

Doing this book was a great joy. It allowed us to work in tandem and deepen a friendship that took roots in the early 1980s. We spent hours together as we wrote and rewrote parts of the book, and discussed each chapter in great detail.

While we sailed through this long voyage, we took help of many friends. To all of them, we owe a big warm thank you. A 'bouquet of thanks' is especially due to:

Mansi Johri, for role-playing many *asanas*, exercises and posture-related dos and don'ts.

Dr Praveen Gulati, Chief of Dr Gulati's Imaging Centre, Hauz Khas Enclave, New Delhi, and his staff for acting out their part in many of the wonderful pictures published in this work.

Dr Kulwant Lohia, Orthopaedic Surgeon; Dr Sheetal Singh, Physiotherapist; and Dr Manisha Kulkarni, Clinical Psychologist, for providing some excellent pictures which are worth their weight in gold.

Ravi and Sonil Singhania, for lending us some wonderful pictures from their personal album.

Hemant Bhatnagar, Art Director, Span; and Abhimanyu Sinha, Senior Illustrator, Hindustan Times, for their creative inputs, which reflect all through this work.

Manju Gupta, for cleaning up the text not once but twice, with a red pencil in hand.

Dilip and Rita, who looked at the draft, gave us time and thought, and enthused us to complete this voyage.

Our patients, without whom this work could not have taken shape, and who remain, our best teachers.

New Delhi

Yatish Agarwal
A P Singh